THE ANTI-CAPITALIST RESISTANCE COMIC BOOK

GORD HILL

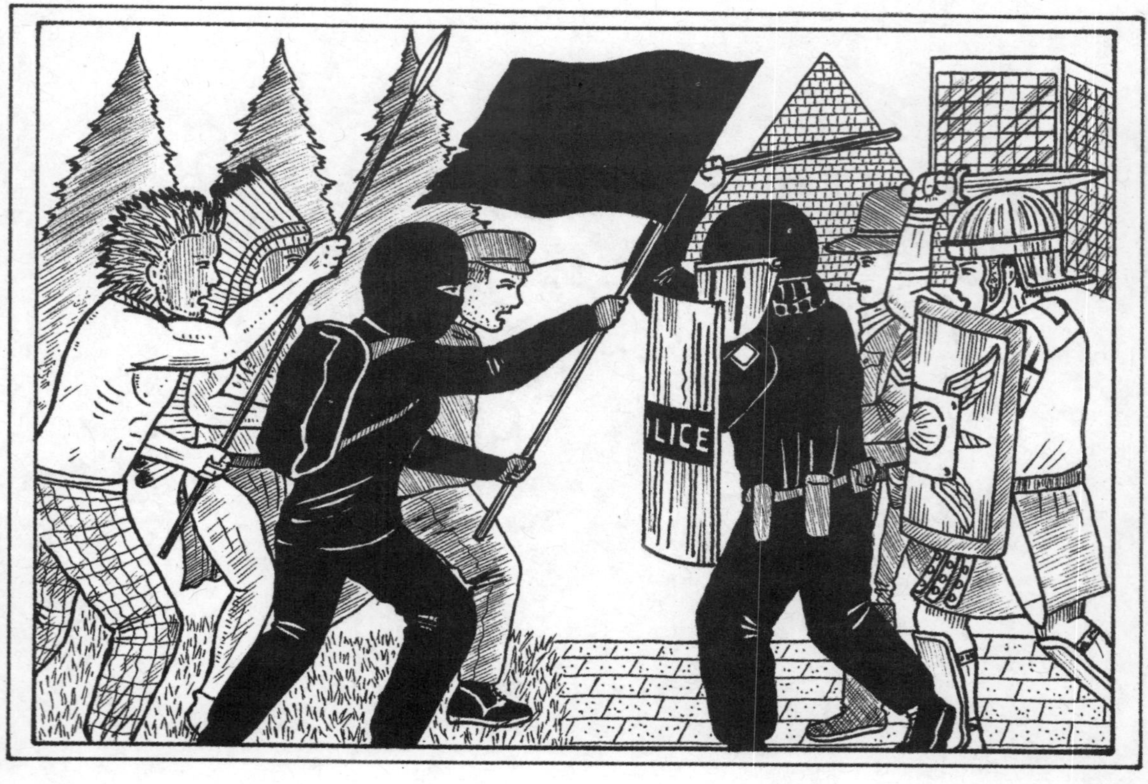
LICE

THE ANTI-CAPITALIST RESISTANCE COMIC BOOK

GORD HILL

ARSENAL
PULP PRESS
VANCOUVER

THE ANTI-CAPITALIST RESISTANCE COMIC BOOK
Copyright © 2012 by Gord Hill
Introduction and Foreword © 2012 by the authors

Second Printing: 2017

ARSENAL PULP PRESS
#202-211 East Georgia St.
Vancouver, BC
Canada V6A 1Z6
arsenalpulp.com

The publisher gratefully acknowledges the support of the Canada Council for the Arts and the British Columbia Arts Council for its publishing program, and the Government of Canada (through the Canada Book Fund) and the Government of British Columbia (through the Book Publishing Tax Credit Program) for its publishing activities.

Printed and bound in Canada

Library and Archives Canada Cataloguing in Publication:

Hill, Gord, 1968-
    The anti-capitalist resistance comic book / Gord Hill.

Also issued in electronic format.
ISBN 978-1-55152-444-3

    1. Anti-globalization movement—Comic books, strips, etc.
2. Capitalism—History—Comic books, strips, etc. 3. Social action—Comic books, strips, etc. 4. Graphic novels. I. Title.

HN17.5.H54 2012   303.48'4   C2012-901137-1

CONTENTS

FOREWORD: The Politics of Rupture

Allan Antliff

Shortly after anarchist-organized disruptions at the G20[1] Summit in Pittsburgh on September 24-25, 2009, the "ex-workers" collective Crimethinc published a comic entitled *Rolling Dumpster*, which described the political radicalization of a garbage bin that goes from feeding vegans to serving as a projectile for the Black Bloc.[2] The story reminded me of a similarly radicalized dumpster I helped to roll down a street during the April 2000 mobilizations against the International Monetary Fund/World Bank in Washington, DC. There, people were already looking ahead to shutting down the June 2000 meetings of the Organization of the American States (OAS) in Windsor, Ontario, Canada.[3] As Windsor, OAS members would prepare the agenda for a "Free Trade Agreement of the Americas" (FTAA) which was to be signed at the third annual Summit of the Americas in Quebec City in April 2001. But that wasn't all that was going on. Washington, DC, Windsor, Quebec City, and Seattle, site of the World Trade Organization (WTO) protests in 1999, would prove to be tactical battlegrounds pitting anarchist-style militancy against government repression, leftist co-optation, and state-corporate media management.

Gord Hill's history reveals that anarchists did not arrive in Seattle devoid of tactics. Our strategic weapons—affinity groups and masking up, human barricades and lockdowns, street theater and other forms of disruption—had all been put into practice before. For example, the Independent Media Center that proved so effective in bypassing corporate news in Seattle was modeled on media centers at "Active Resistance" anarchist gatherings in Chicago (1996) and Toronto (1998).[4] Similarly, as he notes, Black Bloc tactics had been tried out on numerous occasions, including 1992 demonstrations in San Francisco protesting the 500th anniversary of Columbus's invasion of the Americas.[5] Lastly, anarchist modes of non-hierarchical organizing for street confrontations presented state officialdom, corporate media, unions, non-government organizations (NGOs), and the socialist left with a well-honed "fight-back" version of "what democracy looks like."[6] What set it all ablaze was the Zapatistas' "Encuentro for Humanity and Against Neo-liberalism" in Chiapas, Mexico in 1996. This helped to galvanize an international network of Indigenous and non-Indigenous activists to mobilize along explicitly anti-capitalist lines (the Vancouver Asian-Pacific Economic Cooperation Summit was another important catalyst).[7] A second "Encountro" in Spain in 1998 spawned the "People's Global Action" network, which then coordinated a series of international global days of action, notably the "Carnival Against Capitalism" on June 18, 1999, where militant street tactics were part of the mix.[8] As all these elements came together on a mass scale, they drew unions, NGOs, and the left into an anarchist/anti-capitalist protest vortex that escaped control, shaking up the powers-that-be and laying the ground for the wave of disruptions that followed.

Anarchism generated tensions internally and externally. Within the broad-based coalitions making up the anti-capitalist movement, anarchists attacked both capitalism and the state *as such*, a position that upset the usual round of trade-offs and politicking between governments and NGOs or leftist attempts to channel anti-capitalist militancy into statist political programs. For example, at the G20 Summit in Toronto in June 2010, one of Canada's most well-known "progressives," socialist Judy Rebick, was completely caught off-guard by the Black Bloc actions documented in this book.[9] Responding with a post on the website *rabble.ca* (which she cofounded with other left-wing journalists to court an audience among those mobilizing for the 2001 actions in Quebec City), Rebick praised union-organized attempts to direct people away from confrontations and claimed the police had allowed the Black Bloc to succeed in a bid to justify repressing the "overwhelmingly peaceful" mass of demonstrators who, in her political imaginary, were simply asserting their "right to protest ... where political leaders can hear them."[10] Rebick has long pushed for more street-level 'activism' as a supplement to the political program of the Canadian socialist-'lite' New Democratic Party and her hostility towards the Black Bloc is rooted in a deeper desire: to seize the reins of state and replace the existing power hierarchy with one of her own concoction.[11]

While anarchism sharpened the meaning of radicalism within the anti-capitalist movement, externally it was transforming the tenor of protesting, bringing confrontations with corporate and state power to the forefront. In Seattle and again in Washington, DC, activists from the Direct Action Network, a loose coalition of anarchist-influenced groups, organized tactics leftists such as Rebick might grudgingly go along with, such as blockades and lockdowns, in the name of "non-violent direct action." However, when the Black Bloc showed up ready for property destruction and street battles, the ability of this non-violent line to encapsulate what anti-capitalist demonstrating entailed was thrown into question. In response, at their founding meeting on March 25, 2000, organizers of the Windsor OAS Shutdown Coalition (which included Black Bloc participants from Washington, DC) integrated property destruction and respect for diversity of tactics into their "Statement of Principles."[12] This initiative was important, though it would not be tested in Windsor due to intense police repression and the small number of militant demonstrators on hand.[13] It was revisited again during the lead-up to the Summit of the Americas, when the Quebec-based anarchist/anti-capitalist CLAC/CASA (Convergence des Luttes Anti-Capitaliste/le Comite d'Accueil du Sommet des Ameriques) organizations adopted a "diversity of tactics ... ranging from popular education to direct action" and "a confrontational attitude [which] rejects reformist alternatives such as lobbying" as their basis of unity.[14] Declaring "we intend to shut down the Summit of the Americas and to turn the FTAA negotiations into a non-event," CLAC/CASA left no doubt as to the combativeness of the demonstrations to come, and those signing on to their principles were, in effect, endorsing the legitimacy of such actions. Subsequently, acceptance of "diversity of tactics," Black Blocs included, would become an informal litmus test of who stood for what at anti-capitalist demonstrations, Toronto being a case in point.

Faced with protesters who refused to play the game of policing themselves, law enforcement agencies in the US and Canada rolled out their counter-insurgency operations, some of which are discussed in this history.[15] Corporate media also colluded with the police to misrepresent anarchists as mindless thugs with no ostensive political goals or constructive social vision while showcasing intimidating "security" weaponry in a bid to keep the general population in line.[16] Ironically, such actions frequently alienated people from the authorities, as public solidarity with protesters at Quebec City made clear. Tightening up internal logistics in the face of police harassment and infiltration also enabled clandestine actions to flourish, particularly during the anti-2010 Winter Olympics campaign. Repression intensified militancy, which clarified for all concerned what taking on capitalism is really about.

Addressing what he is fighting for, Gord begins his narrative with tribal ways of life prior to the imposition of state power, and rightly so. Indigenous affinities with anarchism reside not only in a shared recognition that state power and exploitation are flip sides of the same coin: decentralizing power so as to renew societal ways of life attuned to nature in all its diversity is the heart of the matter for Indigenous peoples and anarchists alike.[17] Anti-colonialism, then, is integral to the struggle for anarchy as we build the alliances that will dismantle the instruments of state power and capitalist exploitation around the globe.[18]

Allan Antliff, Canada Research Chair in Modern Art at the University of Victoria, Canada, is author of *Anarchist Modernism: Art, Politics, and the First American Avant-Garde* (2001) and *Anarchy and Art: From the Paris Commune to the Fall of the Berlin Wall* (2007) and the editor of *Only a Beginning: An Anarchist Anthology* (2004). Art editor for the interdisciplinary journals *Anarchist Studies* and *Anarchist Developments in Cultural Studies*, he is also Director of the University of Victoria's Anarchist Archive, where he is involved in archival acquisitions and the development of the Archive's Digitization Centre and on-line web resources. In addition, he is a member of the Camas Books and Info Shop Collective (*camas.ca*) and the Victoria Anarchist Bookfair Collective (*victoriaanarchistbookfair.ca*).

Endnotes

1   The G20 "Group of 20" was founded in 2008 and is a shorthand term for summits of political leaders, finance ministers, and central bank governors from the nineteen most economically powerful countries in the world, plus the European Union. It supersedes three earlier formations: the G6, founded in 1975 (Britain, United States, Germany, France, Japan, and Italy), the G7 (1976), which added Canada to the group, and the G8 (1997), which included Russia. G20 members are: Argentina, Australia, Brazil, Canada, China, France, Germany, India, Indonesia, Italy, Japan, Mexico, Republic of Korea, Russia, Saudi Arabia, South Africa, Turkey, United Kingdom, the United States, and the European Union.

2   *Rolling Dumpster: An Anarchist Comic of Dangerous Living* (Crimethinc: Fall, 2009).

3   On the Windsor coalition, see http://web.archive.org/web/20001024214618/ http://www.tao.ca/~stopftaa/about.htm#principles. I discuss the history of the free school in Allan Antliff, "Toronto Anarchist Free School," *Only a Beginning: An Anarchist Anthology*, Allan Antliff, ed. (Vancouver: Arsenal Pulp Press, 2004), 340-341.

4   "Indymedia: Precursors and Birth," *We are Everywhere: The Irresistible Rise of Global Anticapitalism*, Notes from Nowhere Collective, eds. (London: Verso Press, 2003), 231. The 1998 Toronto "Active Resistance" gathering is documented in Allan Antliff, "Active Resistance," *Only a Beginning*, 353-356.

5   David Van Deusen, "Early Clashes, North America, 1988-1999," *The Black Bloc Papers*, David Van Deusen and Xavier Massot of the Green Mountain Anarchist Collective, eds. (Shawnee Mission, KS: Breaking Glass Press, 2010), 34-37.

6   Recent examples of ecologically-inspired anarchist militancy in North America are documented in Leslie James Pickering, *The Earth Liberation Front: 1997-2002* (Portland, OR: Arissa Media Group, 2007) and Ann Hansen, *Direct Action: Memoirs of an Urban Guerrilla* (Toronto: Between the Lines and Oakland, CA: AK Press, 2002). Strategies of the UK-based "Class War Federation" and the Italian Insurrectionists, which both promote illegality and mass uprisings in an urban context, have also been influential. See *Class War: A Decade of Disorder*, Ian Bone, Alan Pullen, and Tim Scargill, eds. (London: Verso Press, 1991) and Alfredo Bonanno, *From Riot to Insurrection: Analysis for an Anarchist Perspective Against Post-Industrial Capitalism* (London: Elephant Editions, 1988).

7   Subcomandante Insurgente Marcos, "Tomorrow Begins Today: Invitation to an Insurrection," *We Are Everywhere*, 34-37 and Andrew Flood, "Dreaming of a Reality

where the Past and the Future meet the Present," *We Are Everywhere*, 74. Anti-APEC demonstrations brought together dissidents from around the Pacific Rim, including an Indigenous Caucus which declared: "We, as Indigenous Nations, believe we have a responsibility to ensure a land base and cultural integrity for all future generations. APEC poses a direct threat to the preservation of Indigenous peoples' rights and resources. One of the issues which is plainly being ignored in the APEC negotiations is the rights of Indigenous peoples. Our identity as Indigenous Nations lies in the connection of our peoples to the land and our traditional resources. APEC threatens to lay waste to the land Indigenous peoples have coexisted with since time immemorial in the name of commercial gain, destroying our culture. The 1997 Peoples' Summit APEC Indigenous Peoples' Caucus will provide the opportunity for the Indigenous Nations of the countries affected to convene and take action in an effort to put a stop to APEC's genocidal negligence of our rights as Indigenous Nations." See "1997 People's Summit on APEC: Daily Summit Communiqué, Issue 9, Friday, November 21, 1997": http://web.archive.org/web/20010619204127/http://vcn.bc.ca/summit/popindex.htm.

8 Actions around the world protesting against the G8 and WTO included disruptions in Birmingham, UK initiated by the anarchist "Reclaim the Streets" organization, which forced G8 leaders to leave the city; "Global Day of Action: Party and Protest Against 'Free Trade' and the WTO, May 1998," *We Are Everywhere*, 102-105. The anarchist politics of "Reclaim the Streets" are discussed in John Jordan, "The Art of Necessity: the subversive imagination of anti-road protest and Reclaim the Streets," *DIY Culture: Party & Protest in Nineties Britain*, George McKay, ed. (London: Verso Press, 1998), 129-151.

9 Rebick is a seasoned player in the Canadian left. Before her union-sponsored appointment in 2002 as the Canadian Auto Workers–Sam Gindin Chair in Social Justice and Democracy at Ryerson University, Toronto, she held a top position in a social issue-oriented NGO and served as the journalistic "voice of the left" for the state-funded Canadian Broadcasting Corporation.

10 Judy Rebick, "Toronto is Burning, or is it?" (June 27, 2010): http://rabble.ca/blogs/bloggers/judes/2010/06/toronto-burning-or-it.

11 In the early 1990s, the Brazilian Workers' Party was her model political movement; lately she has been championing the Bolivian regime of Evo Morales. See Judy Rebick, "Beyond Resistance: Making a Better World in the Here and Now" (2011); http://rabble.ca/news/2011/07/beyond-resistance-part-two-creating-better-world-here-and-now.

12 "Call to Action—OAS Windsor June 4-6: Statement of Principles for the

OAS Shutdown Coalition" (adopted March 25, 2000): http://web.archive.org/
web/20010415021642/http://www.tao.ca/~stopftaa/about.htm#principles. The "Statement of Principles for the OAS Shutdown Coalition" reads as follows:

We are against capitalist globalization. Global capitalism is not new, rather its roots
are deeply imbedded in the history of colonization, white supremacy, patriarchy, ho-
mophobia, ageism, class disparity, the concentration of wealth, ecological destruction,
animal abuse, and the rise of imperialism and the nation state. Agreements like the
"Free Trade Area of the Americas," and organizations like the Organization of American States, are simply a way to make the Americas safe for capitalism, but increasingly
miserable for the non-elites of these nations—and further entrench the domination
of Canada, the United States and other Northern Nations over the countries of the
South.

We are against violence. We acknowledge the need for self-defense when confronted
with the incredible amounts of violence carried out against us by the institutions that
oppress. By violence we do not include property damage or swearing, but do include
comments or behavior that is sexist, ageist, homophobic, racist, classist or otherwise
oppressive. If engaging in property damage and/or self-defense we will strive to take
the necessary measures to avoid causing intentional harm to others.

We acknowledge difference in beliefs and backgrounds, and will strive to work in
solidarity to achieve common goals. We respect the necessity of groups and individu-
als to use diverse forms of direct action when confronting oppression. We will employ
an organizational philosophy based on decentralization, direct democracy, and local
affinity.

We support a confrontational attitude, since we do not think that lobbying can have a
major impact in such biased and undemocratic organizations, in which the interests of
global capitalism dictates policy.

13   Andrea del Moral, "Direct Action Convergences 2000," *The Battle of Seattle; The
New Challenge to Capitalist Globalization*, Eddie Yuen, Geroge Katsiaficas, and Daniel
Burton Rose, eds. (New York: Soft Skull Press, 2001), 277.

14   CLAC/CASA "Basis of Unity," May 17, 2001; http://web.archive.org/
web/20010611102617/http://www.quebec2001.net/principesen.html#pclac.

15   During the lead-up to our successful disruption of the kick-off to the Olympic
torch relay in Victoria, BC, Canada on October 30, 2009, I and other organizers were
harassed by "Integrated Security Unit" police officers who showed up at places of
employment and people's homes (we had a phone tree, so when they knocked on my
door I did not answer).

16   See, for example, Bill Kaufmann, "Disrupters in Cowtown: Calgary mayor says G-8 'anarchists' are in the city, security boosted," *Edmonton Sun*, June 14, 2002: 7.

17   How deep these affinities go can be gauged by American anarchist Voltairine de Cleyre's article on "The Mexican Revolution," published 100 years ago in February, 1912. De Cleyre characterized Indigenous peoples as "invincible haters of author-ity" while calling for anarchists to join the armed struggle of the Yaqui and Moquis to restore their "communistic" way of life, which was far more "a part of nature" than the exploitative "civilization" imposed by the Mexican colonial state; Voltairine de Cleyre, "The Mexican Revolution" (1912*), Anarchy!: An Anthology of Emma Goldman's* Mother Earth, Peter Glassgold, ed. (Washington, D.C.: Counterpoint Press, 2001), 321; 329. In May 1911, Heaudennosaunne (Iroquois Federation) fighters had joined forces with American radicals allied with the Mexican anarchist "Land and Liberty" movement to briefly liberate the Mexican state of Baja California. De Cleyre, who agitated in sup-port of "Land and Liberty" until her untimely death at age forty-six, was undoubtedly aware of these developments. On the Baja insurrection, see James A. Sandos, *Rebel-lion in the Borderlands: Anarchism and the Plan of San Diego, 1904-1923* (Norman, OK: Oklahoma University Press, 1992), 27; De Cleyre's activities in support of "Land and Liberty" are discussed in Paul Avrich, *An American Anarchist: The Life of Voltairine de Cleyre – Anarchist, Feminist, Genius* (Princeton, NJ: Princeton University Press, 1978), 225-231.

18   Peter Gelderloos, *Anarchy Works* (San Francisco: Ardent Press, 2010), 106.

INTRODUCTION

Dave Cunningham

As I write this, it is January 27, 2012 and Tahrir Square in Cairo is again occupied with protesters militantly marking the one-year anniversary of The Day of Rage. The intifada, which continues to blast through the Middle East and Africa, and the ongoing global Occupation's spirit of struggle are the perfect points of departure for the conclusion of activist/artist Gord Hill's latest book. At first glance, it might seem that this is some kind of illustrated anarchist cookbook, or an activist blueprint for what must be done. However, "we don't need a weatherman to tell us which way the wind blows," and thankfully Gord does not position himself as such.

With his appreciation of the nature of social ruptures, Gord leads us along the trajectory of the story of the anti-capitalist movement through its breaks and flows. There is no natural progress from one stage to the next, although the sequential style of the graphic novel creates such a sense of continuum. Rather, Gord manages to slow the cyclones down just long enough for us to peer into the storm. He also returns to us the images that we may have forgotten—those which at the time inspired the ferocity of the struggles depicted here, and which still possess the potential to ignite.

My first encounter with Gord's work was a photocopy (… of a photocopy, of a photocopy …). Like so many other summit-hoppers, I became familiar with Gord's drawings and analysis through his Zig-Zag and Warrior Publications. Now iconic to many, his work circulated through every counter-summit that gathered on Turtle Island (North America) and beyond. It allowed the predominantly white Black Bloc to feel a genuine affinity with warrior culture, and made us seek such a tradition within our own varied and disputed pasts.

I believe it is this affinity, and not just the singular intensity of Gord's spirit, which has allowed his work to avoid the stain of appropriation or tokenism. His work is grounded in his own indigenous struggles, offering white settlers routes for solidarity and lines of flight from colonial mentality. It's as if he dares us to steal this thunder, knowing that no matter what it touches, it will burn.

It was during the cycle of struggle he depicts as the anti-Olympic movement that I found myself in a Vancouver jail cell with Gord for a dozen or so hours; the circumstances that resulted in our capture are featured in the book. Upon our arrival at the jail, we were hauled out of the paddy wagon, and when the screw inspected it he saw the words "RIOT 2010" scrawled on the walls and freaked out. Searching all three of us, the cops discovered that we all possessed black markers.

Alone under the buzzing light of our cell, we passed the time discussing, amongst other stuff, Gord's agit-prop work, both written and graphic. I was startled to discover that he had relied on his illustrative style for pragmatic reasons, specifically because the images photocopied better than DIY-style cut-and-paste photos. As computers became more accessible, he began to use websites and email to disseminate his writing. This proved to be a much more efficient way to get his stuff out there faster, and to many more people. But still, as informative and inflammatory as his written analysis continued to be, we were deprived of the beautifully militant aesthetic of his illustrations, which we had cut our teeth on.

The power of Gord's art is apparent in the series of posters he made during the countdown to the Olympics. Some of these posters became just as disruptive, if not more so, than the demonstrations they were calling for. The first that comes to mind is the one depicting VANOC (the Vancouver Organizing Committee for the 2010 Winter Olympics) as a snake being beheaded, with the caption, "It is elementary to the Art of War: Cut off the head and the body will die!" This incendiary imagery created within the No Olympics Coalition a purifying discussion on the topic of "violence" and "pacifism" (discussed in this book as well).

Another poster from this time depicted the protest against the Olympic flag ceremony, which portrayed said flag on fire. What was cosmically brilliant, and which belies Gord's uncanny ability to anticipate conflict, was that two days before the protest, the flag was stolen from the grounds of Vancouver City Hall. Immediately, Gord's posters which had saturated the city for weeks were juxtaposed with the image of the Native Warrior Society standing with the captured flag—and in turn mobilized one of the largest and rowdiest demos against the Olympic spectacle.

Okay, enough tales. I will save them for the campfires and barricades, where no doubt this comic will be passed around. What makes this book so brutal is that the demarcation between revolt and Empire is drawn with stark, black-and-white contrast. Gord cleaves the civil war that rages both in the streets and within our selves by articulating the front lines that cut across our struggles. Never are we led to believe it is all one movement, nor are we allowed to ignore the contradictions. Always we are reminded of the past, which is cast here not as a dead weight, but an opportunity to avenge.

Thanks to Arsenal for publishing this stuff. The 2010 release of Gord's first book, *The 500 Years of Resistance Comic Book*, was a joyous occasion for all of us acquainted with Gord's work, and I still can't believe it actually got published! It's fitting that the publishers who printed *The Minimanual of the Urban Guerrilla* and *How It All Began*, as well as many other insurrectionary tracts, ended up publishing both *The 500 Years* and now this one.

And in keeping with the concluding image of this book, we scan the horizon for the opening of new potentialities, better able to reflect on our mission for having shared this comic with friends and allies.

Dave Cunningham, an antagonist, settled in the badlands of eastvan, is the author of *Fragments of Intifada: travels in Tunisia & Egypt* and writes on the blog *momentofinsurrection.wordpress.com*

PROLOGUE:
A BRIEF HISTORY OF CAPITALISM

FROM THE EARLIEST CITY-STATES, THE FORCES OF EMPIRE HAVE MARCHED TO TAKE LAND + RESOURCES AND TO IMPOSE THEIR SYSTEM OF CONTROL.

THIS COLONIZATION OF LANDS AND PEOPLE BROUGHT THE CITY-STATES INTO CONFLICT WITH TRIBAL NATIONS. THE ROMAN EMPIRE COLONIZED MOST OF WESTERN EUROPE AND OCCUPIED SOME REGIONS FOR 4-5 CENTURIES.

THESE TWO WAYS OF LIFE — URBAN AND TRIBAL — WERE OPPOSED TO ONE ANOTHER BY THEIR VERY NATURE. CIVILIZATION IN FACT REQUIRED EXPANSION DUE TO RESOURCE DEPLETION + OVER-POPULATION.

TRIBAL SOCIETY LIVED IN ACCORD WITH THE NATURAL WORLD, ORGANIZED IN AUTONOMOUS + DECENTRALIZED VILLAGES. THE EARTH WAS REGARDED AS A MOTHER, AND WOMEN HAD IMPORTANT SOCIAL ROLES...

CIVILIZATION SAW THE EARTH AS SOMETHING TO CONQUER + EXPLOIT. IT WAS ORGANIZED IN A PYRAMID OF POWER, WITH THE ELITE AT THE TOP. WOMEN WERE LITTLE MORE THAN SLAVES IN A PATRIARCHAL SOCIETY.

UNDER ROMAN OCCUPATION, LARGE REGIONS OF TRIBAL PEOPLES WERE INCREASINGLY ASSIMILATED TO THE ROMAN WAY OF LIFE.

CORRUPT WARLORDS, OFTEN IN ALLIANCE WITH THE ROMANS, SUCCEEDED IN TURNING THE TRIBAL PEOPLES INTO PEASANTS, FORCED TO FARM THE LAND...

BY THE 5TH CENTURY THE ROMAN EMPIRE HAD COLLAPSED...

AT THIS TIME, ASSIMILATED TRIBAL CHIEFS ROSE TO ESTABLISH THEIR OWN KINGDOMS, LEADING TO A LONG PERIOD OF WAR AND POWER STRUGGLES UNDER FEUDALISM.

UNDER THE CHURCH, THE LAST REMNANTS OF TRIBAL CULTURE WERE DESTROYED. DURING THE HOLY INQUISITION, MILLIONS OF WOMEN WERE KILLED FOR BEING WITCHES + PAGANS.

THIS DYING EUROPE WAS ONLY REVIVED WITH THE INVASION OF THE AMERICAS, BEGINNING IN 1492 WITH THE VOYAGE OF COLUMBUS TO THE CARIBBEAN REGION.

UNDER THE FEUDAL SYSTEM, FORMER TRIBAL PEOPLES WERE ENSLAVED AS SERFS- PEASANTS FORCED TO WORK THE LAND FOR THE ARISTOCRACY. OVER TIME, AS RESOURCES WERE DEPLETED AND AS POPULATIONS GREW, EUROPE SUFFERED WIDESPREAD POVERTY, DISEASE EPIDEMICS, AND OVERALL SOCIAL DECLINE AND DECAY...

THE CHURCH WAS VITAL IN MAINTAINING THE FEUDAL SYSTEM. A REIGN OF TERROR WAS IMPOSED: THE 'HOLY INQUISITION.'

THE INVASION OF THE AMERICAS BROUGHT NEW RESOURCES TO EUROPE + CREATED NEW MARKETS. MILLIONS OF AFRICANS WERE IMPORTED AS SLAVES FOR MINES, RANCHES, AND PLANTATIONS.

THIS INFUSION OF WEALTH HAD A SIGNIFICANT IMPACT ON EUROPEAN STATES...

EVENTUALLY LEADING TO THE INDUSTRIAL REVOLUTION WITH MACHINES + FACTORIES. PEASANTS WERE FORCED OFF THE LAND TO WORK IN NEW URBAN FACTORIES. REVOLTS REQUIRED MORE + MORE STATE CONTROL TO PREVENT UNREST.

A NEW CLASS OF TRADERS + MERCHANTS EMERGED WHO CHALLENGED THE FEUDAL SYSTEM. THESE WERE THE CAPITALISTS.

THE CAPITALISTS SOUGHT FREE MARKETS + COMPETITION UNRESTRICTED BY FEUDALISM, WHICH CONTROLLED ALL LAND AND TRADE. TENSION BETWEEN CAPITALISTS + FEUDAL RULE INCREASED...

IN 1789 THE FRENCH REVOLUTION OVERTHREW THE MONARCHY AND ESTABLISHED A REPUBLIC - THE STATE NOW BECAME AN INSTRUMENT FOR CAPITALIST EXPANSION + CONTROL.

ALONG WITH A NEW CAPITALIST CLASS, A NEW CLASS OF INDUSTRIAL WORKERS WAS CREATED. TOILING IN THE FACTORIES, THESE WORKERS ORGANIZED + CHALLENGED THE CAPITALISTS. SOME SOUGHT BETTER WORKING CONDITIONS + POLITICAL POWER (THE SOCIAL DEMOCRATS); SOME SOUGHT WORKER CONTROL OF THE STATE (COMMUNISTS); OTHERS PROMOTED THE DESTRUCTION + OVERTHROW OF BOTH CAPITALISM + THE STATE (THE ANARCHISTS)...

BY THE LATE 1800s MOST OF THE WORLD WAS CONTROLLED BY EITHER EUROPEAN STATES OR THE U.S. THE STRUGGLE FOR GLOBAL POWER REACHED ITS PEAK WITH THE OUTBREAK OF WORLD WAR 1, THE FIRST MAJOR INDUSTRIAL WAR WITH TANKS, PLANES, MACHINE GUNS, AND TRENCH WARFARE.

MUCH OF WESTERN EUROPE WAS DEVASTATED BY THE WAR, WITH SOME 25 MILLION PEOPLE DYING. THE U.S., WHICH SAW NO COMBAT ON ITS OWN TERRITORY, EMERGED FROM WW1 IN A FAR STRONGER POSITION THAN ITS EUROPEAN COMPETITORS...

REVOLUTION! ALL POWER TO THE SOVIETS!

EUROPE, ON THE OTHER HAND, SAW RENEWED SOCIAL CONFLICT, WITH A NEAR-REVOLUTION IN GERMANY. IN RUSSIA, SOLDIERS + SAILORS ORGANIZED SOVIETS (COUNCILS) ALONG WITH WORKERS. THEY SUCCEEDED IN OVERTHROWING THE TSAR + ESTABLISHING STATE-CONTROLLED COMMUNISM. THE 1917 RUSSIAN REVOLUTION TERRIFIED THE CAPITALIST RULING CLASSES.

IN 1929, THE STOCK MARKETS COLLAPSED, CAUSING A GLOBAL ECONOMIC CRISIS. MILLIONS LOST THEIR SAVINGS + THEIR JOBS. ARMIES OF UNEMPLOYED POOR PEOPLE APPEARED + SOCIAL CONFLICT INCREASED...

GERMANY, FORCED TO PAY FOR THE COSTS OF WW1, ALREADY SUFFERED POVERTY DURING THE 1920s. THE DEPRESSION MADE CONDITIONS WORSE. THREATENED BY INSURRECTION, A FASCIST STATE WAS IMPOSED UNDER THE CONTROL OF HITLER AND HIS NAZI PARTY. GERMANY BEGAN TO REARM + TAKE INCREASINGLY EXPANSIONIST ACTIONS. BY 1939, THE SECOND WORLD WAR HAD BEGUN. IT ENDED IN 1945 AFTER MASSIVE DESTRUCTION...

AS IN WW1, THE U.S. AGAIN EMERGED MORE POWERFUL, NOW CHALLENGED ONLY BY A GREATLY EXPANDED SOVIET UNION.

WITH EUROPEAN STATES WEAKENED BY WAR, MANY COUNTRIES BEGAN ANTI-COLONIAL REVOLUTIONS, AIDED BY EITHER THE U.S. OR SOVIET UNION...

VIETNAM, ALGERIA, KENYA, MALAYA, + MANY OTHERS SAW WIDESPREAD ARMED REVOLTS, WITH MANY ACHIEVING INDEPENDENCE. BOTH THE U.S. + SOVIETS USED THESE STRUGGLES AS PROXY WARS DURING THE 'COLD WAR'.

A NEW WORLD ORDER!

IN 1989, THE SOVIET UNION COLLAPSED DUE TO A CONVERGENCE OF ECONOMIC, ECOLOGICAL, POLITICAL, MILITARY, + SOCIAL CRISES. WITH THE DEMISE OF THE ONLY COMPETING GLOBAL POWER, THE U.S. BEGAN TO OCCUPY THE OIL-RICH PERSIAN GULF, STARTING WITH THE ATTACK ON IRAQ IN 1990/91.

THE CAPITALIST WEST HAD 'TRIUMPHED' OVER ITS MAIN IDEOLOGICAL RIVAL - THE COMMUNIST BLOC. CAPITALISM HAD WON...

THIS TRIUMPHALISM CONTINUED INTO 1992 WITH CELEBRATIONS OF 500 YEARS SINCE THE INVASION OF THE AMERICAS...

BUT IT WASN'T ALL BAD. IN CANADA, THE 'OKA CRISIS' SAW ARMED MOHAWK WARRIORS RESIST THE POLICE + ARMY IN A 77-DAY STANDOFF THAT INSPIRED NATIVES ACROSS THE LAND. DURING THE SUMMER OF 1990.

IN ECUADOR THAT SAME YEAR, NATIVES FIGHTING FOR THEIR LAND SHUT DOWN THE COUNTRY WITH BLOCKADES OF HIGHWAYS, ROADS + RAILWAYS, PARALYZING THE ECONOMY...

IN 1992, INDIGENOUS PEOPLES + ANTI-COLONIAL ALLIES CONFRONTED COLUMBUS DAY CELEBRATIONS ACROSS THE CONTINENT. IN SAN FRANCISCO, A BLACK BLOC ALSO MARCHED, ONE OF THE EARLIEST IN N. AMERICA.

ON NEW YEARS DAY, 1994, ZAPATISTA GUERRILLAS SEIZED 7 TOWNS IN THE MEXICAN STATE OF CHIAPAS. THEY WERE OPPOSED TO THE NORTH AMERICAN FREE TRADE AGREEMENT (NAFTA).

THEY IDENTIFIED NEO-LIBERALISM AS THE NEW IDEOLOGY OF CAPITALISM.

THE RISE OF ANTI-GLOBALIZATION

NEO-LIBERALISM? PRETTY BIG WORD...

IT JUST MEANS A 'NEW FREEDOM'. WE'RE STUDYING IT IN IN CLASS...

JANUARY 2, 1994: EAST VANCOUVER

"A NEW FREEDOM FOR THE CAPITALISTS AND THEIR CORPORATIONS TO EXPAND, WITH LESS RESTRICTIONS OR REGULATION FROM NATIONAL STATE GOVERNMENTS..."

"IT'S NOW POSSIBLE TO FULLY INTEGRATE THE GLOBAL ECONOMY THANKS TO NEW TECHNOLOGIES IN PRODUCTION + TRANSPORT. IN OTHER WORDS: GLOBALIZATION..."

THAT'S WHAT THE NORTH AMERICAN FREE TRADE AGREEMENT (NAFTA) IS.

THE ZAPATISTAS SAY IT'S A DEATH SENTENCE FOR THE PEASANTS. THAT'S WHY THEY DECLARED WAR!

IT SAYS HERE THAT THE ZAPATISTAS ARE AN INDIGENOUS REBEL ARMY WITH A CLANDESTINE INDIGENOUS COORDINATING COMMITTEE.

YA BASTA!

AN INDIGENOUS REBEL ARMY? THAT IS SO COOL!

YA, IT IS! WELL I GUESS WE SHOULD HEAD DOWNTOWN FOR THE SOLIDARITY RALLY...

IN SOLIDARITY WITH ZAPATISTA REBELLION

THE ZAPATISTAS INSPIRED MOVEMENTS DEMORALIZED BY THE 'VICTORY' OF CAPITALISM. THEY ALSO HELPED FOCUS MANY ON CHANGES OCCURRING IN THE GLOBAL CAPITALIST SYSTEM (i.e., GLOBALIZATION).

IN 1997, VANCOUVER HOSTED THE ASIA-PACIFIC ECONOMIC COOPERATION (APEC) CONFERENCE. OFFICIALS MET TO PLAN THE PLUNDER OF RESOURCES IN THE REGION...

A BROAD ARRAY OF SOCIAL JUSTICE + STUDENT GROUPS MOBILIZED TO PROTEST APEC, WHICH WAS TO BE HELD AT THE UNIVERSITY OF BC...

THEY ORGANIZED FORUMS + RALLIES TO RAISE AWARENESS ABOUT APEC...

TARGET'S ENTERING A CAFE...

THE RCMP CONDUCTED SURVEILLANCE ON ORGANIZERS, TAPPED PHONES, USED INFIL-TRATORS, + ARRESTED SOME...

DURING THE CONFERENCE, HUNDREDS OF COPS WERE DEPLOYED. PROTESTERS TORE DOWN SECTIONS OF CROWD CONTROL FENCING, WHILE POLICE USED PEPPER SPRAY TO CLEAR A ROAD USED BY APEC DELEGATES. THE INCIDENT BECAME KNOWN AS 'SPRAYPEC' AND LED TO A GOVERNMENT INQUIRY...

J18: GLOBAL
CARNIVAL AGAINST CAPITAL

THE GLOBAL CARNIVAL AGAINST CAPITAL TOOK PLACE JUNE 18, 1999, ALSO KNOWN AS "J18."

RECLAIM THE STREETS

IT COINCIDED WITH THE 25TH G8 SUMMIT IN COLOGNE, GERMANY + WAS INSPIRED BY ACTIONS AT THE 1998 G8 SUMMIT IN BIRMINGHAM, UK.

IN LONDON, RADICALS PREPARED FOR MANY MONTHS TO ORGANIZE + PROMOTE THE CARNIVAL.

GLOBAL CARN

A PROMO VIDEO WAS PRODUCED, 10,000 POSTERS + STICKERS MADE, + 4,000 COPIES OF A MAP WITH CORPORATE TARGETS DISTRIBUTED.

ON JUNE 18, 30,000 COPIES OF A SPOOF EDITION OF THE EVENING STANDARD WERE HANDED OUT, HEADLINED "GLOBAL MARKET MELTDOWN."

EVENING STANDARDS

GLOBAL MARKET MELTDOWN!

10,000 MASKS WERE GIVEN OUT WITH A FLYER: "THOSE IN POWER FEAR THE MASK FOR THEIR POWER PARTLY RESIDES IN...KNOWING WHO YOU ARE.

"...OUR MASKS ARE NOT TO CONCEAL OUR IDENTITY BUT TO REVEAL IT... TODAY WE SHALL GIVE THIS RESISTANCE A FACE..."

BETWEEN 5-10,000 PARTICIPATED IN LONDON ON J18. THEIR NUMBERS + MILITANCY OVERWHELMED POLICE + THERE WAS EXTENSIVE DAMAGE TO CORPORATE BUSINESSES + BANKS...

J18 TOOK PLACE IN OVER 40 COUNTRIES + WAS ONE OF THE FIRST MAJOR GLOBAL ANTI-CAPITALIST PROTESTS.

MAKE OUR RESISTANCE AS GLOBAL AS CAPITALISM!

MANY MILITANTS + RADICALS WERE INSPIRED BY J18 + CARRIED THIS ENTHUSIASM WITH THEM INTO SEATTLE 5 MONTHS LATER...

THE BATTLE IN SEATTLE
SHUTTING DOWN THE W.T.O.

SURE, MAYBE THE '90s HADN'T STARTED SO GREAT, BUT IT SURE ENDED WITH A BANG...

LOTS OF BANGS, ACTUALLY, FROM TEAR GAS TO CONCUSSION GRENADES AND RUBBER BULLETS!

THE WORLD TRADE ORGANIZATION (WTO) WAS ESTABLISHED IN 1995 AS A GLOBAL COURT. DOMINATED BY THE U.S. + ITS ALLIES, THE WTO MAKES DECISIONS ON TRADE DISPUTES ARISING FROM THE NEO-LIBERAL SYSTEM...

THE WTO MEETING IN SEATTLE FROM NOV. 1-3, 1999, DREW THE WRATH OF A BROAD RANGE OF SOCIAL MOVEMENTS: LABOUR, ENVIRON-MENTALISTS, INDIGENOUS, ANTI-CAPITALISTS...

ORGANIZING THE MASS PROTESTS BEGAN A YEAR EARLIER. FORUMS, NEWSLETTERS, POSTERS, + SPEAKING TOURS WERE USED TO EDUCATE + MOBILIZE PEOPLE TO CONVERGE IN SEATTLE.

BY 1999, THE INTERNET WAS WIDELY USED FOR MASS MOBILIZING. AS PART OF ANTI-WTO ORGANIZING, THE FIRST INDEPENDENT MEDIA CENTER (IMC) WAS ESTABLISHED...

MANY NON-GOVERNMENTAL ORGANIZATIONS (NGOs) + GRASSROOTS GROUPS TRAINED PEOPLE FOR CIVIL DISOBEDIENCE IN THE STREETS...

STREET MEDICS TRAINED FOR INJURIES FROM TEAR GAS, PEPPER SPRAY AND BATONS...

WHILE NGOs CALLED FOR INCLUSION IN THE WTO MEETINGS, MORE RADICAL GROUPS CALLED FOR A SHUTDOWN. MOST ADVOCATED PACIFIST METHODS...

SOME MILITANTS HAD A MORE TACTFUL APPROACH IN MIND, HOWEVER...

MEANWHILE, IN BELLA COOLA, A REMOTE NATIVE COMMUNITY ON THE CENTRAL COAST OF B.C....

SO YOU REALLY THINK IT'LL BE A BIG DEAL? I NEVER EVEN HEARD OF THE WTO!

OH HELL YA!!

GROUPS HAVE BEEN PREPARING FOR, LIKE, A YEAR NOW. IF PEOPLE HAVEN'T HEARD OF THE WTO, THEY SURE WILL AFTER THIS...

AND IT WON'T BE AS A GOOD THING!

NOV. 27, 1999.

JUST REMEMBER: IF YOU SEE ANY COPS, STAY LOW!

OK, "DAD"!

SLAM!

JEEZ! 2 DAYS STUCK IN THE BACK OF THIS TRUCK...

YA-BUT IT'LL BE WORTH IT!

NOV. 29, 1999

RISE AND SHINE! WE'RE IN SEATTLE!

AFTER BREAKFAST, LET'S CHECK OUT THE D.A.N. SPACE!

"DAN"? WHO'S HE?

MAN, YOU'RE REALLY OUTTA THE LOOP ON THIS ONE...

D.A.N. IS THE DIRECT ACTION NETWORK. THEY HAVE A CONVERGENCE SPACE UP IN THE CAPITOL HILL DISTRICT.

LATER, AT THE DAN CONVERVGENCE CENTER...

THEY'RE HAVING A SPOKESCOUNCIL ABOUT TOMORROW'S PROTEST ACTIONS.

HHMPH! IT DOESN'T LOOK ALL THAT BIG TO ME!

THESE ARE JUST DELEGATES FROM SOME OF THE AFFINITY GROUPS.

THAT DAY THERE WERE SEVERAL PROTESTS AGAINST THE WTO + GLOBALIZATION, AS THERE HAD BEEN ALL WEEK.

WTO! HELL NO! FIGHT BACK

ANOTHER WORLD IS POSSIBLE!

NOV. 30, 7 AM: THOUSANDS OF PROTESTERS DESCENDED ON THE DOWNTOWN CORE...

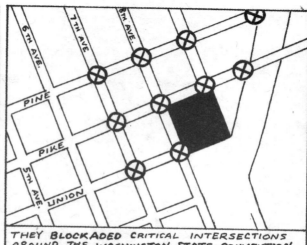

THEY BLOCKADED CRITICAL INTERSECTIONS AROUND THE WASHINGTON STATE CONVENTION CENTER, SITE OF THE WTO TALKS...

A WIDE VARIETY OF MATERIALS WERE USED IN THE BLOCKADES...

LOCKBOXES AND TRIPODS...

PUPPETS + BARRELS OF CONCRETE...

CARS AND DUMPSTERS...

AND SHEER MASSES OF PEOPLE IN THE STREETS...

DESPITE THE BLOCKADES, A CARNIVAL LIKE ATMOSPHERE PREVAILED...

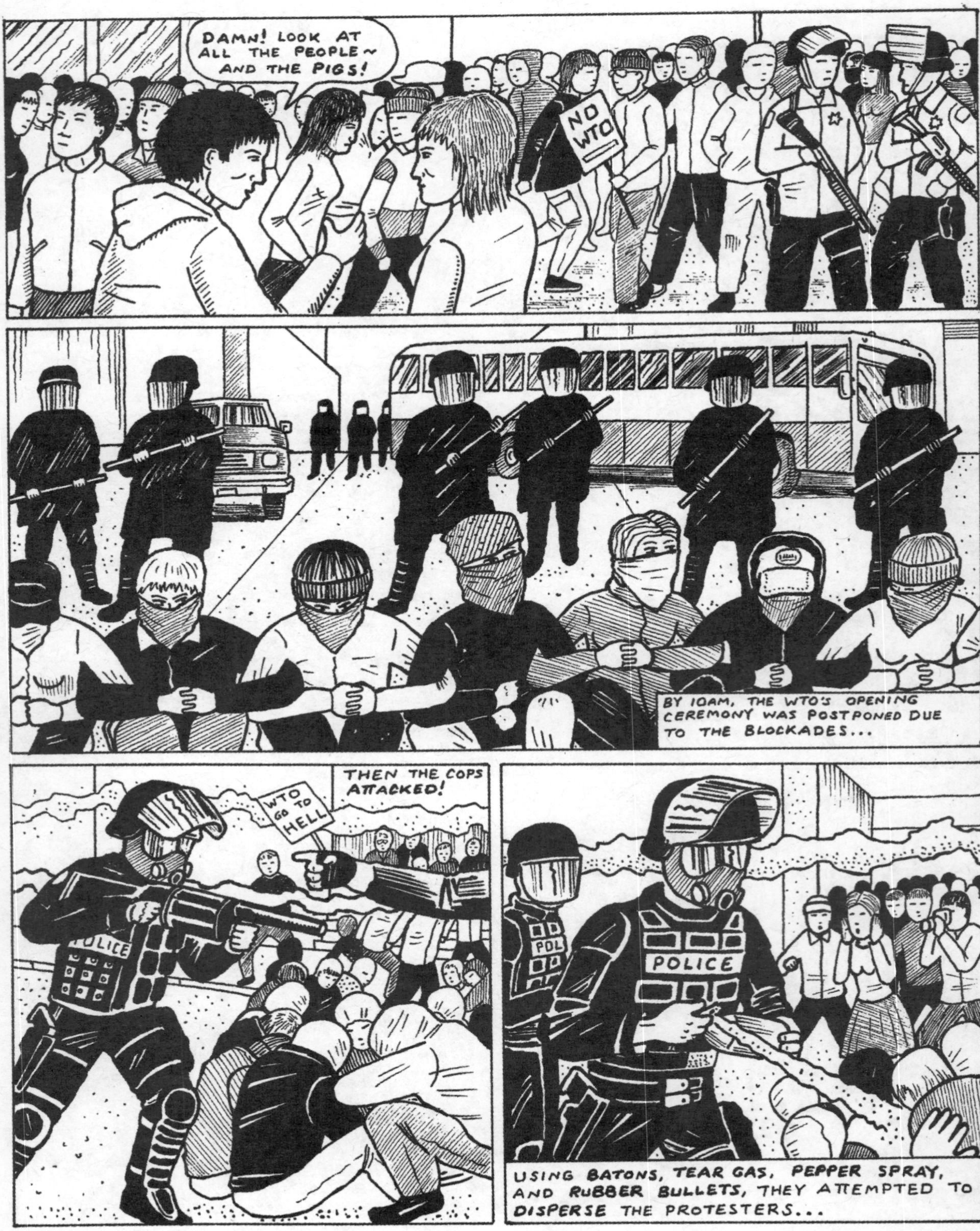
DAMN! LOOK AT ALL THE PEOPLE~ AND THE PIGS!
NO WTO
BY 10AM, THE WTO'S OPENING CEREMONY WAS POSTPONED DUE TO THE BLOCKADES...
THEN THE COPS ATTACKED!
WTO GO TO HELL
POLICE
PDL
POLICE
USING BATONS, TEAR GAS, PEPPER SPRAY, AND RUBBER BULLETS, THEY ATTEMPTED TO DISPERSE THE PROTESTERS...

BUT THE CROWDS WERE FAR TOO LARGE...

AGITATED BY THE COPS' ASSAULT, PROTESTERS BEGAN THROWING BACK TEAR GAS CANISTERS.

SOME BEGAN REINFORCING THE BLOCKADES AND BUILDING NEW ONES...

SEVERAL WERE SET ON FIRE.

MEANWHILE, IN ANOTHER PART OF THE CITY, AND AWAY FROM THE SITES OF CIVIL DISOBEDIENCE ACTIONS, A BLACK BLOC OF LESS THAN 50 GATHERED + TOOK TO THE STREETS.

CKS

KRASH!

TIME

SMASH!

THEY ATTACKED THE PROPERTY OF CORPORATE STOREFRONTS, INCLUDING McDONALD'S, NIKETOWN, BANK OF AMERICA, STARBUCKS, LEVIS, THE GAP, AS WELL AS CORPORATE MEDIA EQUIPMENT AND POLICE CARS...

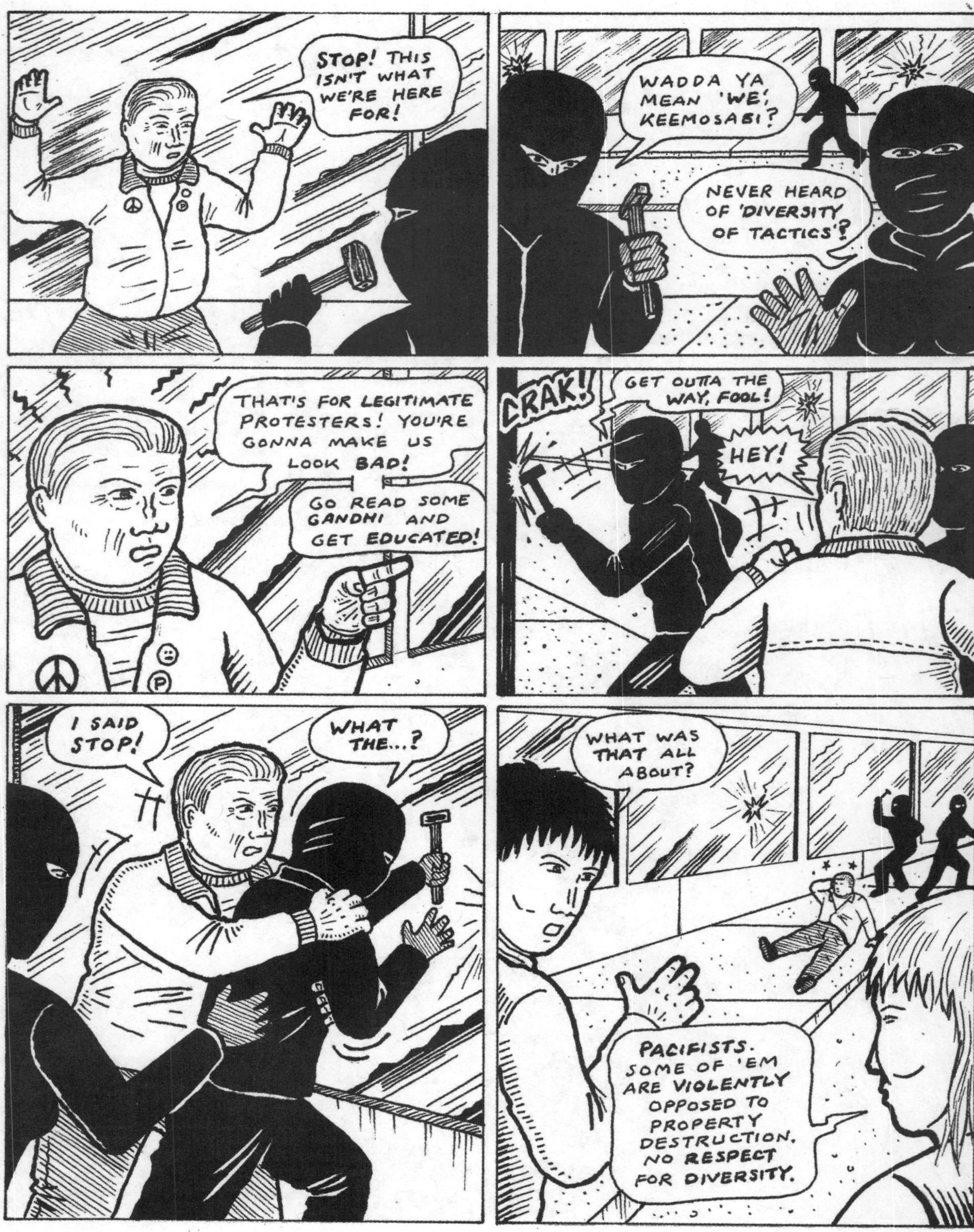

STOP! THIS ISN'T WHAT WE'RE HERE FOR!
WADDA YA MEAN 'WE', KEEMOSABI?
NEVER HEARD OF 'DIVERSITY OF TACTICS'?
THAT'S FOR LEGITIMATE PROTESTERS! YOU'RE GONNA MAKE US LOOK BAD!
GO READ SOME GANDHI AND GET EDUCATED!
CRAK!
GET OUTTA THE WAY, FOOL!
HEY!
I SAID STOP!
WHAT THE...?
WHAT WAS THAT ALL ABOUT?
PACIFISTS. SOME OF 'EM ARE VIOLENTLY OPPOSED TO PROPERTY DESTRUCTION. NO RESPECT FOR DIVERSITY.

EARLIER IN THE DAY, AT AROUND 10 AM, 20,000 HAD GATHERED FOR A LABOUR RALLY AT THE SEATTLE CENTER...

ORGANIZERS MET WITH POLICE + GOVERNMENT OFFICIALS...

THEIR PLAN WAS TO MARCH DOWNTOWN, THEN BACK TO THE SEATTLE CENTER — HERDING AS MANY PROTESTERS AS POSSIBLE AWAY FROM THE DIRECT ACTIONS...

INSTEAD, SEVERAL THOUSAND LEFT THE PARADE TO JOIN THE BLOCKADES...

BY 1PM, THE WTO'S OPENING CEREMONIES WERE CANCELLED, ALONG WITH MANY OF ITS MEETINGS...

AT 3:30 PM, A STATE OF EMERGENCY WAS DECLARED, AUTHORIZING THE USE OF TROOPS FROM THE NATIONAL GUARD AS WELL AS A 7PM TO 7AM CURFEW IN THE DOWNTOWN.

IN THE EARLY EVENING, POLICE SUCCEEDED IN FORCING MOST OF THE PROTESTERS OUT OF THE DOWNTOWN AND INTO THE CAPITOL HILL DISTRICT...

RIOTING OCCURRED INTO THE EARLY MORNING, WITH MANY LOCAL RESIDENTS PARTICIPATING.

AT 7AM THE NEXT DAY, THOUSANDS OF PEOPLE ONCE AGAIN ASSEMBLED IN THE DOWNTOWN AND BEGAN BLOCKADING THE STREETS.

SEVERAL HUNDRED NATIONAL GUARD TROOPS REINFORCED THE POLICE. A 'NO PROTEST' ZONE WAS IMPOSED AROUND THE WTO SITE; GAS MASKS + PICKET SIGNS WERE BANNED.

BY 7:30 AM THE POLICE BEGAN MASS ARRESTS.

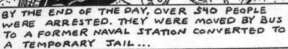

BY THE END OF THE DAY, OVER 540 PEOPLE WERE ARRESTED. THEY WERE MOVED BY BUS TO A FORMER NAVAL STATION CONVERTED TO A TEMPORARY JAIL...

MANY REFUSED TO LEAVE THE BUSES AND MOST DID NOT IDENTIFY THEMSELVES. THESE TACTICS SLOWED DOWN THE ARREST PROCESS.

BEGINNING IN THE AFTERNOON, POLICE WITHDREW FROM THE BLOCKADES TO FOCUS ON THE ARRIVAL OF U.S. PRESIDENT CLINTON AND HIS MOTORCADE TO THE WTO MEETINGS.

AT 4PM, AS CLINTON DEPARTED, THE COPS RESUMED THEIR ATTACKS ON PROTESTERS.

AT 6:45PM, MOST OF THE DOWNTOWN BLOCKADES WERE VOLUNTARILY ABANDONED TO AVOID THE 7PM—7AM CURFEW.

WITH THE DOWNTOWN CLEARED, POLICE RACED THROUGH THE STREETS IN CONVOYS, A TACTIC OF INTIMIDATION THEY CALLED 'WILD WEASEL'. (THEIR ARMOURED VEHICLES WERE 'PEACEMAKERS').

ONCE AGAIN, THOUSANDS OF PROTESTERS WITHDREW TO THE CAPITOL HILL DISTRICT.

AT 9:30 PM, POLICE BEGAN A RAMPAGE IN THE CAPITOL HILL, SEEMINGLY IN A RAGE BECAUSE THEY COULDN'T CONTROL THE STREETS.

MANY OF THESE ASSAULTS WOULD RESULT IN CIVIL LAWSUITS AGAINST THE POLICE...

ONE MAN WAS SHOT IN THE CHEST WITH A 'BEAN BAG' ROUND AT CLOSE RANGE...

TWO JOURNALISM STUDENTS FILMING FROM THEIR CAR WERE APPROACHED BY A COP. HE MOTIONED TO THEM TO LOWER THEIR WINDOW, AND WHEN THEY DID...

ON THURSDAY, DEC. 2, AND FOR 2 DAYS AFTER, JAIL SOLIDARITY BECAME THE MAIN FOCUS OF PROTESTS, AT TIMES SURROUNDING THE SEATTLE PUBLIC SAFETY BUILDING, WHERE MANY PRISONERS WERE BEING HELD.

BY SUNDAY, MOST OF THE PRISONERS WERE RELEASED, THE RESULT OF JAIL SOLIDARITY ACTIONS + NEGOTIATIONS. BY JANUARY 2000, OVER 90% OF CHARGES WERE DROPPED.

SEATTLE POLICE CHIEF NORM STAMPER AND SEVERAL OTHER SENIOR OFFICERS RESIGNED IN THE MONTHS FOLLOWING, THE RESULT OF SIGNIFICANT PUBLIC CRITICISM OF POLICE.

THE SEATTLE PROTESTS SUCCESSFULLY DISRUPTED THE WTO MEETINGS AND INSPIRED A NEW GENERATION OF SOCIAL MOVEMENTS. FUTURE ANTI-CAPITALIST ACTIONS MODELLED THEMSELVES ON THE ANTI-WTO CONVERGENCE...

SUMMIT OF THE AMERICAS
QUEBEC CITY 2001

FROM APRIL 20-22, 2001, QUEBEC CITY HOSTED THE SUMMIT OF THE AMERICAS. 34 HEADS OF STATE WERE TO NEGOTIATE THE FREE TRADE AREA OF THE AMERICAS (FTAA).

APPROPRIATELY, THE SUMMIT WAS TO BE IN THE CITADEL, AN OLD FORTRESS WITH A HISTORY OF WAR, AND IMPERIAL EXPANSION.

AFTER THE SEATTLE ANTI-WTO CONVERGENCE, THE ANTI-CAPITALIST RESISTANCE IN BOTH EUROPE + NORTH AMERICA EXPANDED...

MAKE CAPITALISM HISTORY

IN JANUARY 2000-CLASHES IN DAVOS, SWITZERLAND, AGAINST THE WORLD ECONOMIC FORUM, IN APRIL AGAINST THE IMF/WB IN WASHINGTON, DC, AND IN SEPTEMBER AGAINST THE IMF/WB IN PRAGUE, CZECH REPUBLIC.

WITH THE EXCEPTION OF DAVOS, THESE WERE MASS MOBILIZATIONS INVOLVING TENS OF THOUSANDS. THEY ALSO SAW STRONGER DISPLAYS OF MILITANCY, INCLUDING THE FORMING OF BLACK BLOCS.

DRESSED IN UNIFORM ALL-BLACK CLOTHING, THE BLACK BLOC COUNTERED SURVEILLANCE AND ENABLED MILITANTS TO ACT. INSIDE THE BLOC WERE AFFINITY GROUPS- GROUPS OF COMRADES WHO SHARED THE SAME GOALS, TACTICS, AND METHODS.

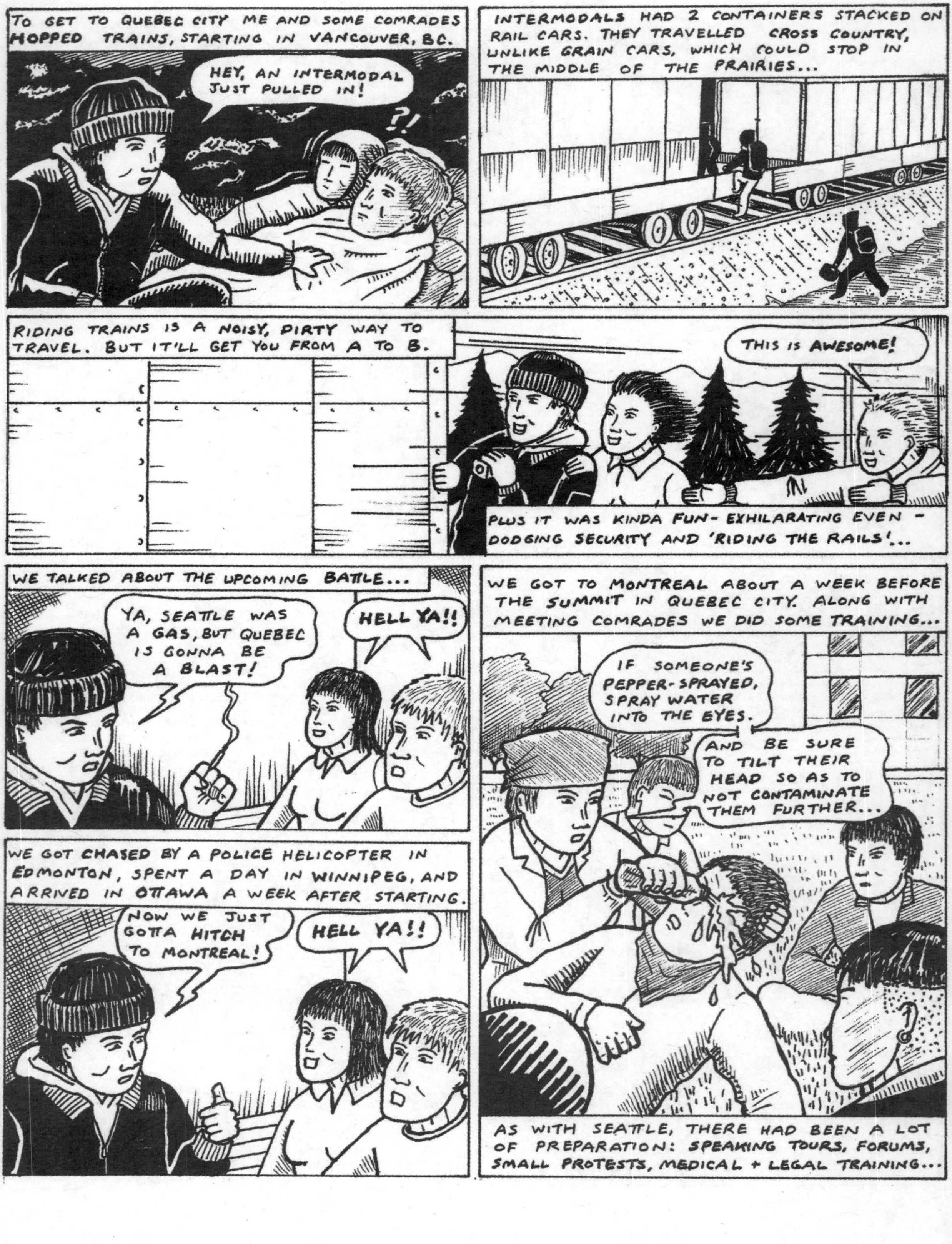

TO GET TO QUEBEC CITY ME AND SOME COMRADES HOPPED TRAINS, STARTING IN VANCOUVER, B.C.
HEY, AN INTERMODAL JUST PULLED IN!
?!
INTERMODALS HAD 2 CONTAINERS STACKED ON RAIL CARS. THEY TRAVELLED CROSS COUNTRY, UNLIKE GRAIN CARS, WHICH COULD STOP IN THE MIDDLE OF THE PRAIRIES...
RIDING TRAINS IS A NOISY, DIRTY WAY TO TRAVEL. BUT IT'LL GET YOU FROM A TO B.
THIS IS AWESOME!
PLUS IT WAS KINDA FUN- EXHILARATING EVEN - DODGING SECURITY AND 'RIDING THE RAILS'...
WE TALKED ABOUT THE UPCOMING BATTLE...
YA, SEATTLE WAS A GAS, BUT QUEBEC IS GONNA BE A BLAST!
HELL YA!!
WE GOT CHASED BY A POLICE HELICOPTER IN EDMONTON, SPENT A DAY IN WINNIPEG, AND ARRIVED IN OTTAWA A WEEK AFTER STARTING.
NOW WE JUST GOTTA HITCH TO MONTREAL!
HELL YA!!
WE GOT TO MONTREAL ABOUT A WEEK BEFORE THE SUMMIT IN QUEBEC CITY. ALONG WITH MEETING COMRADES WE DID SOME TRAINING...
IF SOMEONE'S PEPPER-SPRAYED, SPRAY WATER INTO THE EYES.
AND BE SURE TO TILT THEIR HEAD SO AS TO NOT CONTAMINATE THEM FURTHER...
AS WITH SEATTLE, THERE HAD BEEN A LOT OF PREPARATION: SPEAKING TOURS, FORUMS, SMALL PROTESTS, MEDICAL + LEGAL TRAINING...

WE MET A GROUP OF *STUDENTS* PREPARING FOR THE SUMMIT. THEY WERE RADICAL BUT HAD A VERY DIM VIEW OF MARCHING IN A BLACK BLOC.

MARCHING IN A BLACK BLOC IS SUICIDAL!

WE'VE BUILT THESE SUITS TO PROTECT US BUT THEY'RE MORE THEATRICAL + LESS THREATENING...

WE WEREN'T IMPRESSED...

THEY LOOK LIKE CLOWNS!

RIDICULOUS!

LET'S GET MORE BEER!

HELL YA!

WITH THEIR OVER-PADDED COSTUMES, THE STUDENT GROUP WERE CLEARLY SCARED BY THE GOVERNMENT PROPAGANDA...

"IF YOU WANT *PEACE*, PREPARE FOR *WAR*," THE QUEBEC SECURITY MINISTER HAD ANNOUNCED. ALONG WITH GRIM WARNINGS ABOUT ANARCHISTS, THEY HAD MOBILIZED SOME 6,000 COPS AND BUILT A 4-KM-LONG FENCE AROUND THE SITE OF THE SUMMIT IN QUEBEC CITY. THE LOCKDOWN GREATLY ANGERED MANY LOCAL RESIDENTS, WE'D LEARNED...

41

ONE OF THE MAIN GROUPS ORGANIZING AGAINST THE SUMMIT WAS THE ANTI-CAPITALIST CONVERGENCE, CLAC IN ITS FRENCH ACRONYM...

THE CLAC WAS A REVOLUTIONARY GROUP THAT HAD A STRONG, COHERENT ANALYSIS AGAINST THE SUMMIT AND CAPITALISM.

OUR GOAL IS TO SHUT DOWN THE SUMMIT!

AND THE MOST MILITANT GOAL...

THE CLAC HAD CHARTERED BUSES TO MOVE PEOPLE FROM MONTREAL TO QUEBEC CITY. WE GOT ONE ON APRIL 18...

...AND ARRIVED LATE THAT EVENING. WE STAYED AT A SCHOOL GYMNASIUM, WHILE OTHERS WERE PUT UP IN COMMUNITY CENTERS, CHURCHES, AND PRIVATE RESIDENCES...

ON APRIL 19, THE NIGHT BEFORE THE SUMMIT, A RALLY WAS HELD. AT FIRST THERE WERE ONLY 300 PEOPLE BUT IT GREW TO OVER 3,000.

IT WAS PEACEFUL + ENDED WITH A BIG STREET PARTY AT 'GRAFFITI PARK'.

THE NEXT DAY— APRIL 20 — WAS THE 'CARNIVAL AGAINST CAPITALISM', CALLED BY CLAC. WE GATHERED AT LAVAL UNIVERSITY.

WE CAN GET READY IN THE UNIVERSITY GYM!

WE WERE GEARING UP TO MARCH IN A BLACK BLOC.

PASS THE DUCT TAPE.

WHILE WE WERE IN MONTREAL WE HAD FOUND MORE COMRADES FOR OUR AFFINITY GROUP.

LET'S GO FIND THE BLACK BLOC!

THE BLACK BLOC HAD BEEN CALLED BY THE REVOLUTIONARY ANTI-CAPITALIST OFFENSIVE.

WE WERE TO FIND THEIR BANNER AND HAD TO PUSH OUR WAY THROUGH THE THOUSANDS THAT HAD GATHERED. WE GRABBED ON TO THE PACK OF THE COMRADE IN FRONT TO STAY TOGETHER.

IT WAS A RELIEF TO FIND THE BANNER~ AS MANY AS 500 IN THE BLACK BLOC. SOME WERE STILL PUTTING ON THEIR PROTECTIVE GEAR (PADDING, HELMETS, SHIN GUARDS, ETC.).

OH HELL YA!

DOES THIS PADDING MAKE ME LOOK FAT?

VIVA LA RESISTA

FUCK OFF WITH THE CAMERA!

REVOLUTIONA ANTI-CAPITALI OFFENSIVE

IT WAS A WARM, SUNNY DAY AND WE WAITED 2 HOURS OR SO BEFORE THE MARCH BEGAN.

PASS THE H2O, BRO'!

HEY-THE MARCH HAS STARTED!

EVEN AFTER IT STARTED IT STILL TOOK TIME BEFORE THE BLACK BLOC STARTED MOVING...

KEEP TIGHT! STAY TOGETHER!

WE HAD TO MARCH MANY BLOCKS TO GET TO THE DOWNTOWN SITE OF THE SUMMIT...

HELL YA!

SMASH!

EN ROUTE, A GAS STATION WAS ATTACKED.

A COP CAR HAD ITS TIRES SLASHED; WHEN THE COP PURSUED MILITANTS INTO THE BLOC HE SUFFERED A BROKEN JAW...

SMASH!

AT A MAJOR INTERSECTION WE WERE TOLD MORE SPECIFIC ROUTES TO MARCH...

RED ZONE - GO RIGHT! GREEN ZONE GO LEFT!

RED WAS CONFRONTATIONAL, GREEN PACIFIST...

ONE OF THE CLAC MEMBERS CHASTISED THE BLOC FOR ITS LACK OF CHANTS + SLOGANS.

WHY SO QUIET BLACK BLOC? CAT GOT YOUR TONGUE?

IT WAS ONE OF THE QUIETEST BLOCS I'D BEEN ON - WE WERE PROBABLY ALL IN DEEP THOUGHT ABOUT THE UPCOMING BATTLE...

AS WE NEARED THE SECURITY PERIMETER FENCE, HOCKEY PUCKS WERE DISTRIBUTED...

HERE ARE SOME PUCKS TO START THE THROWING!

THEN WE FINALLY REACHED THE FENCE...

...IT IMMEDIATELY BEGAN TO BUCKLE.

WITHIN MINUTES A LARGE SECTION OF IT WAS THROWN OVER AND WE SURGED FORWARD.

LET'S GO!

THERE WERE ONLY A FEW RIOT COPS AT THIS LOCATION AND THEY IMMEDIATELY RETREATED.

WE CHASED THEM A BLOCK OR SO, SOME THROWING PROJECTILES.

THEN A PLATOON OF RIOT COPS APPEARED. WE RETREATED TO THE BROKEN FENCING AND BEGAN TEARING UP SLABS OF CONCRETE...

THESE WERE SMASHED TO MAKE PROJECTILES.

MEANWHILE, VEHICLES OF CORPORATE MEDIA OUTSIDE THE FENCE WERE SMASHED.

AT THE FRONT, CHUNKS OF CONCRETE, PUCKS, CUE BALLS + BOTTLES RAINED DOWN ON THE COPS.

THROWING AT AN ANGLE CAUGHT SOME COPS OFF GUARD.

PAINT BOMBS WERE ALSO USED TO OBSCURE THE VISION OF THE COPS' VISORS + SHIELDS.

45

A GROUP OF MILITANTS TOOK A SECTION OF FENCING + CHARGED THE POLICE LINE, THROWING IT INTO THEIR RANKS...

MORE RIOT COPS APPEARED - BOTH QUEBEC POLICE AND RCMP (ROYAL CANADIAN MOUNTED POLICE).

OH GREAT! THERE'S MORE OF THEM!

THEN THE TEAR GAS WAS DEPLOYED - LOTS OF TEAR GAS...

MILITANTS WITH GAS MASKS MOVED FORWARD TO THROW BACK THE TEAR GAS CANISTERS...

THEN ARWEN (ANTI-RIOT WEAPON) GUNNERS STARTED FIRING RUBBER BULLETS.

A GROUP OF MILITANTS MOVED UP WITH SMALL SHIELDS, BUT ONE OF THEM WAS HIT...

MEDIC!

HIS COMRADES CARRIED HIM TO SAFETY...

BY NOW, THE BLACK BLOC WAS DISPERSED AMONG THE THOUSANDS OF PROTESTERS, WHILE STREET FIGHTING OCCURRED OVER A WIDE AREA OF THE CITY.

HEY! IT'S THOSE STUDENTS!

THEY LOOK BEAT!

THOSE SUITS ARE TOO HEAVY...

MUST BE DAMN HOT!

MOVING 1-2 BLOCKS AWAY FROM THE FRONT WE WERE ABLE TO REST, ALTHOUGH THE SITUATION WAS VERY FLUID + COULD CHANGE VERY FAST...

AS WE WANDERED THROUGH THE SIDE STREETS:

LOOK AT THAT! IT'S ABANDONED!

IT'S ONE OF THOSE RENTAL VANS THE RIOT COPS ARE USING.

WE SHOULD SMASH THOSE SHOTGUNS!

BUT JUST AS WE CONTEMPLATED OUR OPTIONS...

HERE COMES THE CAVALRY!

SCREECH!

WE TOOK OFF, THEN SAW GROUPS OF YOUTH WALKING AROUND WITH SHIELDS TAKEN FROM THE ABANDONED VAN...

CHECK THOSE KIDS OUT!

HA!

POLICE POLICE

BECAUSE OF THE FIGHTING, LARGE AREAS OF THE CITY HAD BECOME TEMPORARY AUTONOMOUS ZONES.

THERE WERE NO COPS AWAY FROM THE FENCING, AND EVERYWHERE PEOPLE WERE CELEBRATING AND PARTYING LIKE IT WAS 1999...

LATER IN THE AFTERNOON WE WENT BACK TO THE FRONTLINE - THE SECURITY PERIMETER FENCE.

THE BATTLE WAS STILL RAGING, WITH GROUPS TEARING DOWN SECTIONS OF FENCING USING ROPES AND CARABINERS.

A POLICE WATER CANNON ADVANCED AT ONE POINT, PUSHING BACK THE PROTESTERS...

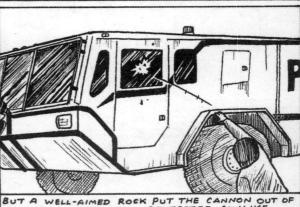

BUT A WELL-AIMED ROCK PUT THE CANNON OUT OF ACTION, ITS WINDOWS UNPROTECTED (UNLIKE WATER CANNONS IN OTHER PARTS OF THE WORLD).

OTHERS CONTINUED TO CLASH WITH RIOT COPS. ONE GROUP CHARGED POLICE AND THREW A SECTION OF METAL FENCING AT THEM...

AND THEN ATTACKED WITH STICKS.

AS EVENING APPROACHED...

MAN- I'M HUNGRY + THIRSTY!

LET'S HIT GRAFFITI PARK AND GET SOME FOOD!

WE GRABBED SOME BEERS AND WENT TO THE PARK. HUNDREDS OF OTHER PROTESTERS HAD ALSO GATHERED...

TODAY WAS AWESOME!

YA- AND THERE'S STILL TOMORROW!

THE NEXT DAY- APRIL 21- WAS THE BIG *NGO* AND *LABOUR* MARCH.

SMALL GROUPS OF BLACK BLOC GATHERED ALONG THE ROUTE, LATER JOINING TOGETHER.

WE WAITED QUITE AWHILE BEFORE JOINING- THERE WERE SOME 60,000 PEOPLE MARCHING.

FUCK OFF WITH THE CAMERA!

AT OUR GROUP'S RALLY POINT SOME REPORTERS HAD THEIR CAMERAS *SMASHED*.

FINALLY WE JOINED THE MARCH, ALTHOUGH AFTER A FEW BLOCKS WE BROKE AWAY TO HEAD TOWARDS THE FENCE...

Québec

AS WE MARCHED, HUNDREDS OF CITIZENS LINING THE STREET CHEERED US LIKE A *LIBERATING ARMY!*

AS SOON AS WE HIT A SECTION OF FENCE IT WAS *BREACHED*, FIRST WITH *BOLT CUTTERS* TO CUT HOLES IN IT.

KOMATSU

AS THE FENCE WAS *TORN AWAY*, A FRONT-END LOADER PARKED AT THE SPOT- A WEAK POINT- WAS DEMOLISHED.

AS WE BROKE THROUGH THE FENCE, 5-6 COPS ON THE OTHER SIDE FLED IN FEAR...

IT'S THE BLACK BLOC! RETREAT!

THEY WERE QUICKLY REINFORCED BY A PLATOON OF COPS, HOWEVER, AND WE SCRAMBLED TO GET BACK THROUGH THE HOLE IN THE FENCE.

MOVE IT!

COMING THROUGH!

AS WE CONTINUED ON, ATTACKING THE FENCE AT OTHER LOCATIONS, WE SMASHED UP A BANK- NOT KNOWING IT WAS IN A 'GREEN ZONE'...

KRASH!

NON!

FUCK YOU HIPPIE!

THE PACIFISTS FREAKED OUT, WITH SOME PROTECTING THE BANK...

OTHER MOBS OF MILITANTS PROWLED THE STREETS, ATTACKING THE FENCE OR COPS.

SEVERAL MOLOTOV COCKTAILS WERE ALSO THROWN.

DESPITE THE LEVEL OF CONFLICT, MANY RESIDENTS SUPPORTED THE MILITANTS.

BY LATE AFTERNOON, POLICE BEGAN TO PUSH OUT FROM AROUND THE FENCE IN AN EFFORT TO CLEAR THE STREETS.

GET OFF THE STREET!

THEY ALSO BEGAN ADVANCING ON THE MEDICAL STATION SET UP TO TREAT INJURED PROTESTERS AND THE NEARBY INDYMEDIA CENTER...

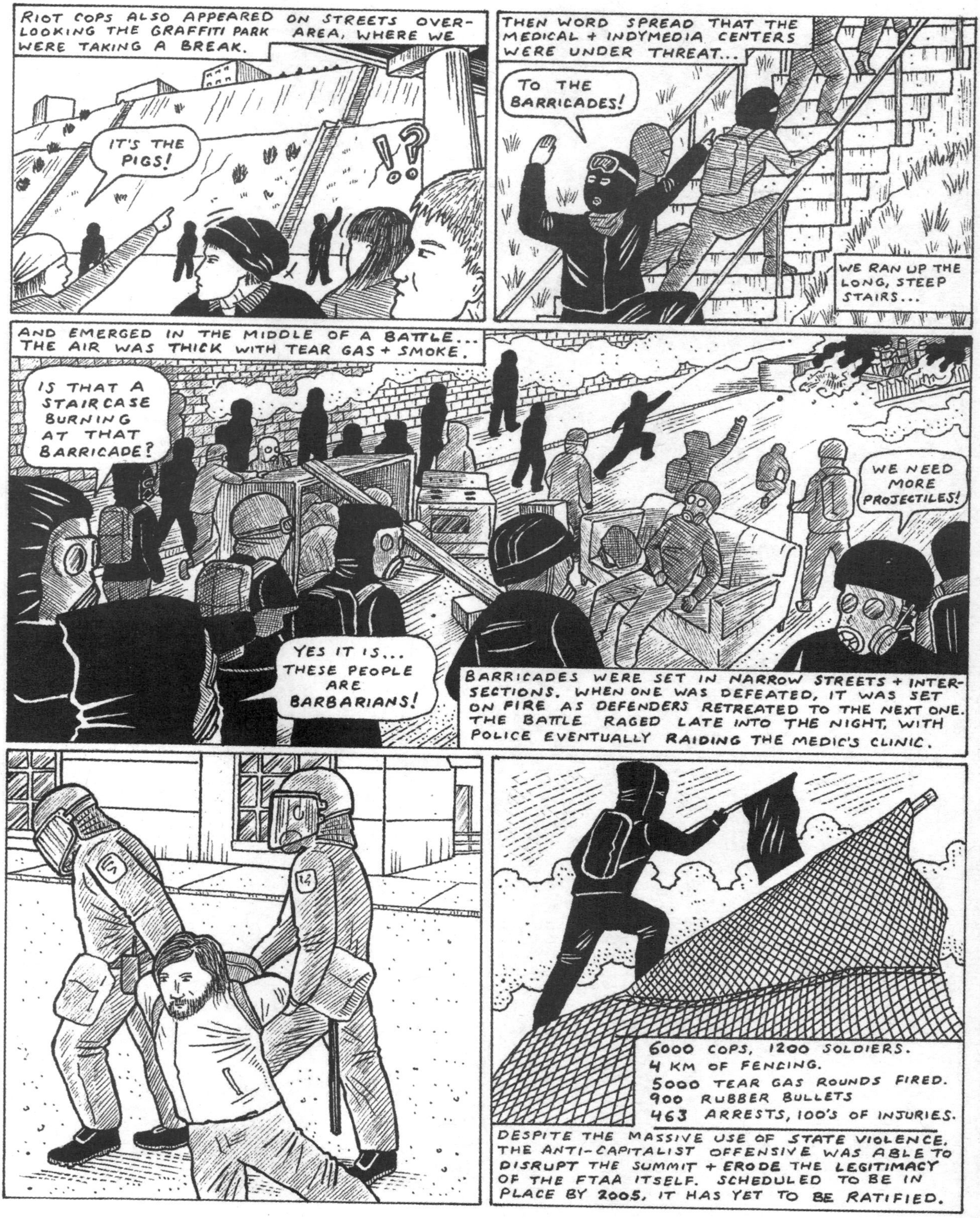

RIOT COPS ALSO APPEARED ON STREETS OVERLOOKING THE GRAFFITI PARK AREA, WHERE WE WERE TAKING A BREAK.
IT'S THE PIGS!
!?
THEN WORD SPREAD THAT THE MEDICAL + INDYMEDIA CENTERS WERE UNDER THREAT...
TO THE BARRICADES!
WE RAN UP THE LONG, STEEP STAIRS...
AND EMERGED IN THE MIDDLE OF A BATTLE... THE AIR WAS THICK WITH TEAR GAS + SMOKE.
IS THAT A STAIRCASE BURNING AT THAT BARRICADE?
YES IT IS... THESE PEOPLE ARE BARBARIANS!
WE NEED MORE PROJECTILES!
BARRICADES WERE SET IN NARROW STREETS + INTERSECTIONS. WHEN ONE WAS DEFEATED, IT WAS SET ON FIRE AS DEFENDERS RETREATED TO THE NEXT ONE. THE BATTLE RAGED LATE INTO THE NIGHT, WITH POLICE EVENTUALLY RAIDING THE MEDIC'S CLINIC.
6000 COPS, 1200 SOLDIERS.
4 KM OF FENCING.
5000 TEAR GAS ROUNDS FIRED.
900 RUBBER BULLETS
463 ARRESTS, 100'S OF INJURIES.
DESPITE THE MASSIVE USE OF STATE VIOLENCE, THE ANTI-CAPITALIST OFFENSIVE WAS ABLE TO DISRUPT THE SUMMIT + ERODE THE LEGITIMACY OF THE FTAA ITSELF. SCHEDULED TO BE IN PLACE BY 2005, IT HAS YET TO BE RATIFIED.

2001: THE RISE AND FALL

OF RADICAL ANTI-CAPITALIST RESISTANCE

AFTER QUEBEC CITY, THE RADICAL ANTI-CAPIT-ALIST RESISTANCE CONTINUED TO GROW ALONG WITH THE 'ANTI-GLOBALIZATION' STRUGGLE.

ON JUNE 15, 2001, IN GOTHENBURG, SWEDEN, MILITANTS CARRIED OUT EXTENSIVE PROPERTY DAMAGE DURING PROTESTS OF THE EUROPEAN UNION.

DURING THE FIGHTING, POLICE OPENED FIRE ON MILITANTS, INJURING 3 (1 SERIOUSLY), AND ARRESTED 1,130 PEOPLE.

ON JULY 20, 2001, IN GENOA, ITALY, SOME 300,000 MARCHED AGAINST THE G8 SUMMIT.

DESPITE A LARGE ARMY OF THOUSANDS OF COPS, THERE WERE EXTENSIVE CLASHES WITH MILITANTS.

ONE MILITANT, 23-YEAR-OLD CARLO GIULIANI, WAS SHOT IN THE HEAD + KILLED BY A COP. GENOA IS CONSIDERED THE PEAK POINT OF THE 'ANTI-GLOBALIZATION' MOVEMENT.

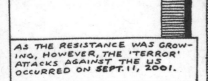

BOOM!

AS THE RESISTANCE WAS GROW-ING, HOWEVER, THE 'TERROR' ATTACKS AGAINST THE US OCCURRED ON SEPT. 11, 2001.

UNDER THE PRETEXT OF A 'WAR ON TERROR', STATES VASTLY EXPANDED THEIR SECURITY FORCES. NEW ANTI-TERROR LAWS WERE QUICKLY PASSED...

THE CLIMATE OF PATRIOTISM AND REPRESSION HAD A CHILLING EFFECT ON SOCIAL MOVEMENTS WITHIN G8 STATES, ONE THAT WOULD TAKE SEVERAL YEARS TO OVERCOME.

ROSTOCK 2007
MILITANT CAMPAIGN AGAINST G8

AFTER THE INSURRECTIONARY PROTESTS OF 2001, AND THE POLICE STATES IMPOSED AFTER 9/11, WTO + G8 SUMMITS SHIFTED TO REMOTE + INACCESSIBLE LOCATIONS.

THESE INCL. QATAR, KANANASKIS (CANADA), CANCUN (MEXICO), AND GLENEAGLES (SCOTLAND).

PROTESTS AGAINST THE FTAA IN MIAMI, 2003, SAW 20,000 DEMONSTRATORS BUT A DEMORALIZING DISPLAY OF POLICE VIOLENCE + CONTROL.

AS MANY AS 200,000 MARCHED IN EDINBURGH IN 2005 AGAINST THE G8 SUMMIT THAT YEAR.

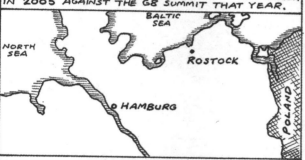

BUT IT WASN'T REALLY UNTIL THE G8 SUMMIT OF 2007, NEAR ROSTOCK, GERMANY, THAT A MILITANT ANTI-CAPITALIST FORCE RE-EMERGED.

2 YEARS BEFORE THE SUMMIT, A 'MILITANT CAMPAIGN AGAINST THE G8' WAS STARTED.

WHO ARE THEY TO DECIDE OUR FUTURE? STOP the G8

IT CONSISTED OF ATTACKS ON CORPORATE, POLICE, MILITARY + GOVERNMENT BUILDINGS, HOMES, AND ESPECIALLY VEHICLES...

ARSON ATTACKS EXPANDED TO INCLUDE LUXURY CARS IN GENERAL. IN THE FIRST 6 MONTHS OF 2007, OVER 100 VEHICLES WERE TORCHED IN BERLIN ALONE...

THE CAMPAIGN WAS, IN PART, A CRITIQUE OF THE LIMITED SCOPE OF THE SUMMIT/COUNTER-SUMMIT MODEL + THE NEED FOR CONTINUOUS RESISTANCE.

THE GERMAN STATE RESPONDED WITH A SERIES OF RAIDS, EXTENSIVE SURVEILLANCE, + ARRESTS, ALL OF WHICH INCREASED AS THE G8 SUMMIT NEARED.

THE ACTUAL G8 SUMMIT WAS JUNE 6-8 IN THE RESORT TOWN OF HEILIGENDAMM, NEAR ROSTOCK.

FOR SECURITY, 16,000 COPS, WITH APC'S, WATER CANNONS, HELICOPTERS + HORSES, WERE DEPLOYED, ALONG WITH 1,000 SOLDIERS + 12 KM OF FENCING.

ROSTOCK ITSELF HAD BECOME INFAMOUS IN 1992 WHEN NEO-NAZIS RIOTED FOR 3 DAYS, ATTACKING A REFUGEE + IMMIGRANT SHELTER COMPLEX.

POLICE WERE CRITICIZED FOR THEIR WEAK EFFORTS IN PREVENTING THE RACIST VIOLENCE.

THE FIRST BIG ANTI-G8 PROTEST OCCURRED ON JUNE 2, 2007, WHICH SAW A BLACK BLOC OF SOME 5,000 MARCHING.

Kampf

80,000 PEOPLE PARTICIPATED IN THE PROTESTS, WITH MANY COMING FROM ACROSS EUROPE.

DEPRIVED OF CORPORATE TARGETS IN THE FORTIFIED COMMERCIAL DISTRICT, MILITANTS CONCENTRATED THEIR ATTACKS ON THE POLICE.

DURING CLASHES, 433 COPS WERE INJURED, MOST FROM PROJECTILES. OVER 500 PROTESTERS WERE ALSO INJURED + OVER 1000 ARRESTED.

ON JUNE 5-6 BLOCKADES WERE SET UP AROUND HEILIGENDAMM, FORCING JOURNALISTS + OTHERS TO TRAVEL BY BOAT TO THE G8 SITE.

POLICE USED BATONS, PEPPER SPRAY, + WATER CANNONS TO CLEAR PEACEFUL PROTESTERS FROM ROADS AND AWAY FROM THE SECURITY FENCE.

MEANWHILE, MILITANTS BUILT BARRICADES ON ROADS + RAILWAY TRACKS AND ALSO DIS-MANTLED SECTIONS OF THE FENCE ITSELF.

THE 'MILITANT CAMPAIGN AGAINST THE G8' SHOWED THAT ANTI-CAPITALIST RESISTANCE WAS STILL A POTENT FORCE WITHIN G8 STATES.

NO 2010
THE ANTI-OLYMPIC CAMPAIGN

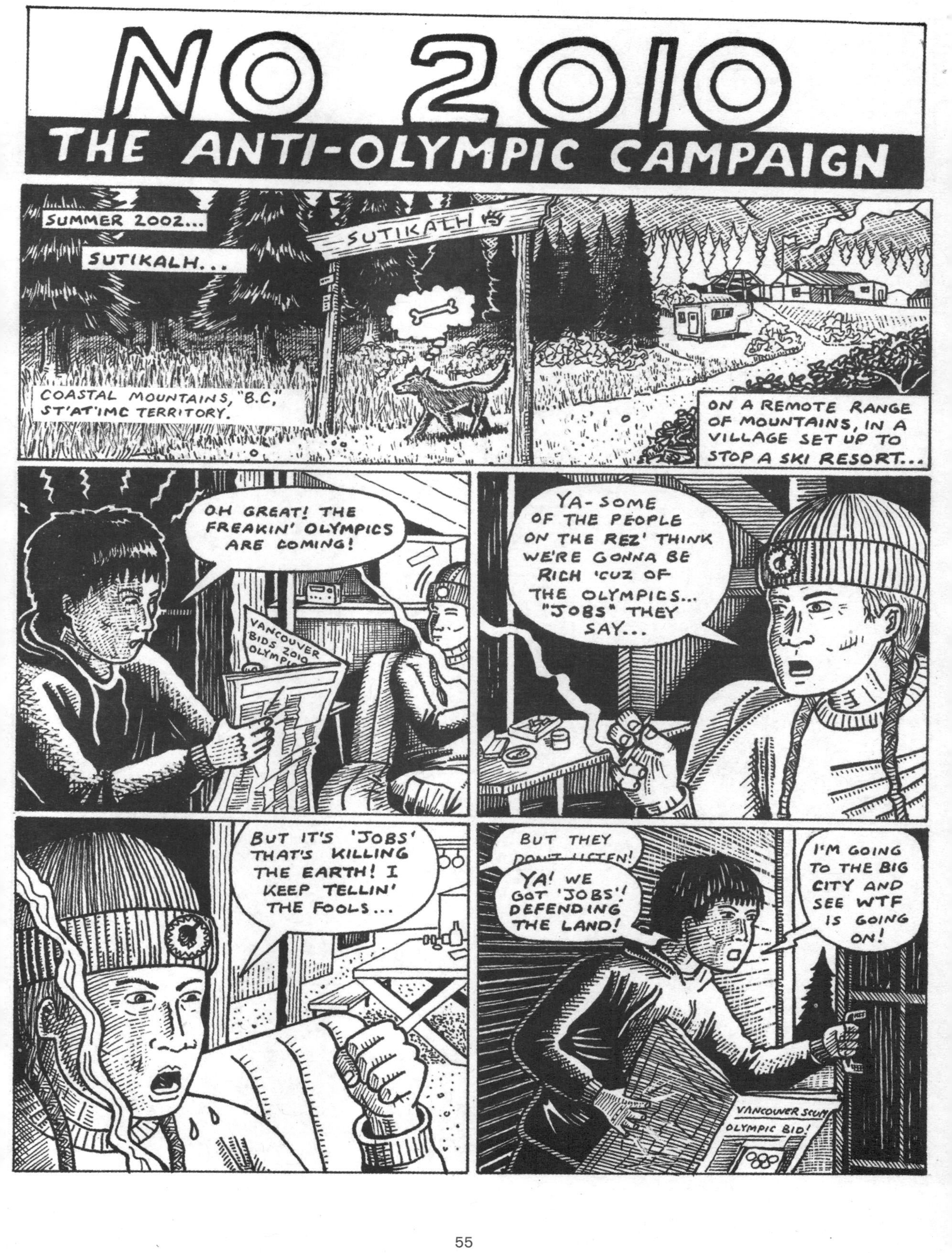

SUMMER 2002...
SUTIKALH...
SUTIKALH
COASTAL MOUNTAINS, "B.C," ST'AT'IMC TERRITORY.
ON A REMOTE RANGE OF MOUNTAINS, IN A VILLAGE SET UP TO STOP A SKI RESORT...
OH GREAT! THE FREAKIN' OLYMPICS ARE COMING!
VANCOUVER BIDS 2010 OLYMPI
YA-SOME OF THE PEOPLE ON THE REZ' THINK WE'RE GONNA BE RICH 'CUZ OF THE OLYMPICS... "JOBS" THEY SAY...
BUT IT'S 'JOBS' THAT'S KILLING THE EARTH! I KEEP TELLIN' THE FOOLS...
BUT THEY DON'T LISTEN!
YA! WE GOT 'JOBS'! DEFENDING THE LAND!
I'M GOING TO THE BIG CITY AND SEE WTF IS GOING ON!
VANCOUVER SCUM
OLYMPIC BID!

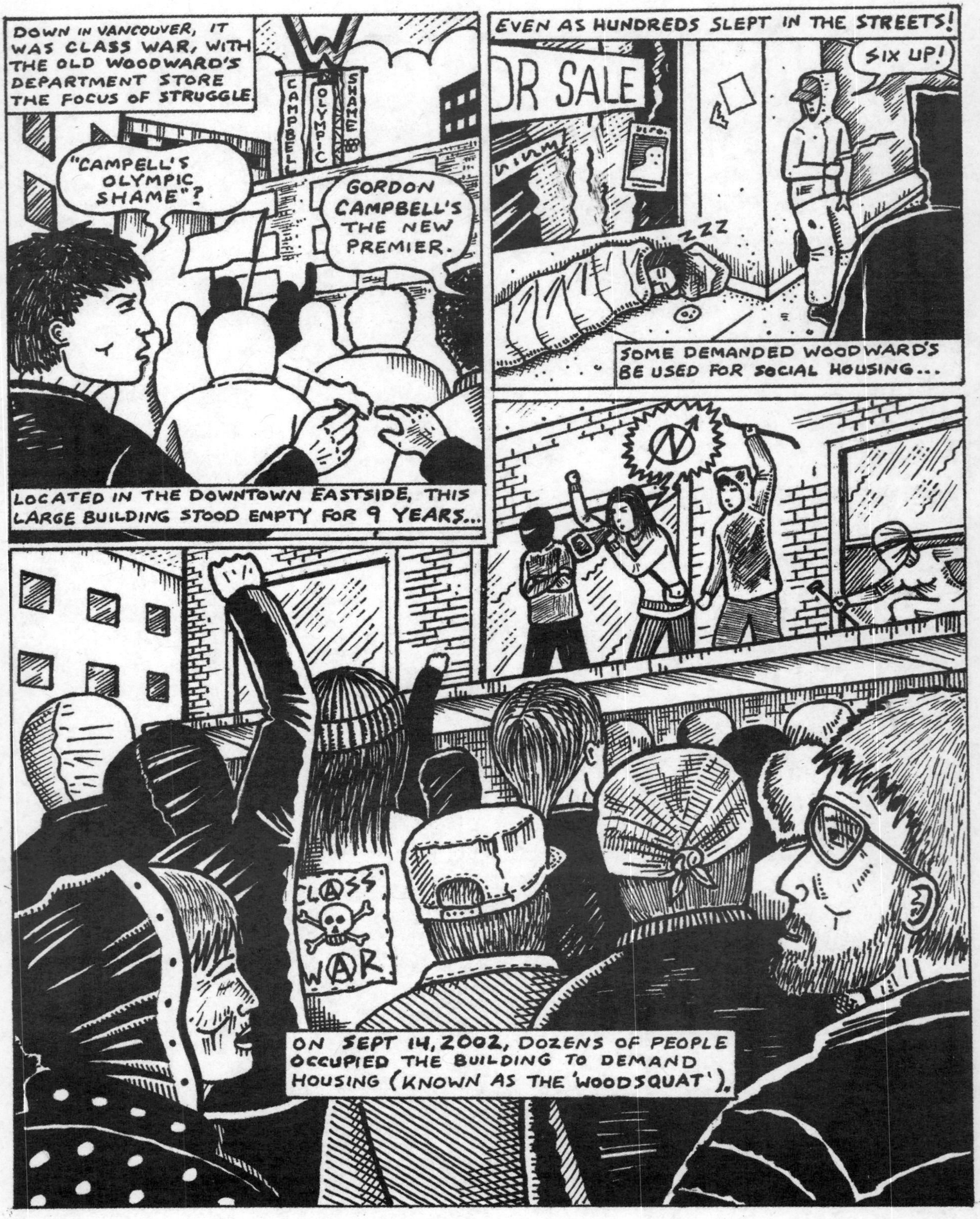
DOWN IN VANCOUVER, IT WAS CLASS WAR, WITH THE OLD WOODWARD'S DEPARTMENT STORE THE FOCUS OF STRUGGLE.
CAMPBELL
OLYMPIC
SHAME
"CAMPELL'S OLYMPIC SHAME"?
GORDON CAMPBELL'S THE NEW PREMIER.
LOCATED IN THE DOWNTOWN EASTSIDE, THIS LARGE BUILDING STOOD EMPTY FOR 9 YEARS...
EVEN AS HUNDREDS SLEPT IN THE STREETS!
OR SALE
SIX UP!
ZZZ
SOME DEMANDED WOODWARD'S BE USED FOR SOCIAL HOUSING...
CLASS WAR
ON SEPT 14, 2002, DOZENS OF PEOPLE OCCUPIED THE BUILDING TO DEMAND HOUSING (KNOWN AS THE 'WOODSQUAT').

INSIDE, THE SQUATTERS ORGANIZED THEIR FOOD, SECURITY, SANITATION, ETC. BUT ON SEPT. 19, AFTER A COURT INJUNCTION WAS ISSUED, OVER 100 COPS RAIDED THE SQUAT.

EVERYONE ON THEIR KNEES!

ACK!

AAGH!

STOP RESISTING ARREST!

I'M NOT-YOU STUPID PIG!!

POLICE

POLICE BROKE THRU' BARRICADED DOORS AND ARRESTED 58 PEOPLE. MANY WERE BEATEN, CHOKED, AND DRAGGED OUT.

THE EVICTED SQUATTERS SET UP A 'TENT CITY' ON SIDEWALKS AROUND WOODWARD'S.

OR SALE

Realtor

WELCOME TO THE BEST PLACE ON EARTH.*

APC

FUCK THE POLICE!

Jesus Slay

HOMES NOT GAMES!

HA! LA LUCHA CONTINUA ~ AMIGO!

THE TENT CITY WOULD LAST 3 MONTHS AND ENDED AFTER AN INJUNCTION AND NEW CITY COUNCIL TOOK POWER. 60 HOMELESS PEOPLE GOT TEMPORARY HOUSING AS A RESULT...

* OFFICIAL BC TOURISM SLOGAN

JULY 1, 2003, EAST VANCOUVER...

SO THE SQUATTERS WON? THAT'S GREAT!

NOT EXACTLY...

THIS KID'S SO NAIVE!

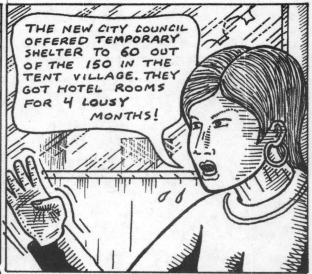

THE NEW CITY COUNCIL OFFERED TEMPORARY SHELTER TO 60 OUT OF THE 150 IN THE TENT VILLAGE. THEY GOT HOTEL ROOMS FOR 4 LOUSY MONTHS!

THEN THEY SAID 200 OUT OF 500 UNITS TO BE BUILT ON THE SITE WOULD BE FOR SOCIAL HOUSING... I DOUBT THAT MANY WILL BE BUILT...

"THE BID CORPORATION—MADE UP OF REAL ESTATE, TOURISM, RESORT AND HOTEL OWNERS, ALONG WITH THE GOVERNMENT, SPENT $5 MILLION ON A 'YES' CAMPAIGN..."

EXTRA! EXTRA! VOTE 'YES'! IT WON'T COST A CENT AND WE'LL ALL BE RICH!

THESE PEOPLE ARE SO NAIVE!

KIEWIT

STOLEN PROVINCE

$6 BILLION

BE A GOOD CITIZEN: VOTE YES

2010 OLYMP.

BLAH JOBS BS BLA BLA

THE NEW MAYOR— LARRY CAMPBELL—A FORMER CORONER AND COP(!) HAD ALSO PLEDGED TO HOLD A PLEBISCITE ON THE OLYMPIC BID. ONCE HE WAS MAYOR, HE WATERED IT DOWN TO A NON-BINDING REFERENDUM...

"IT WAS ANOTHER SCAM! LESS THAN 50% OF THE CITY'S VOTERS TOOK PART. 64% VOTED 'YES', WHILE 36% VOTED 'NO'. BUT THE REFERENDUM SHOULD'VE BEEN PROVINCIAL, AND BINDING! IN THE END JUST 12% OF THE POPULATION WERE INCLUDED, AND ONLY 3% VOTED YES!"

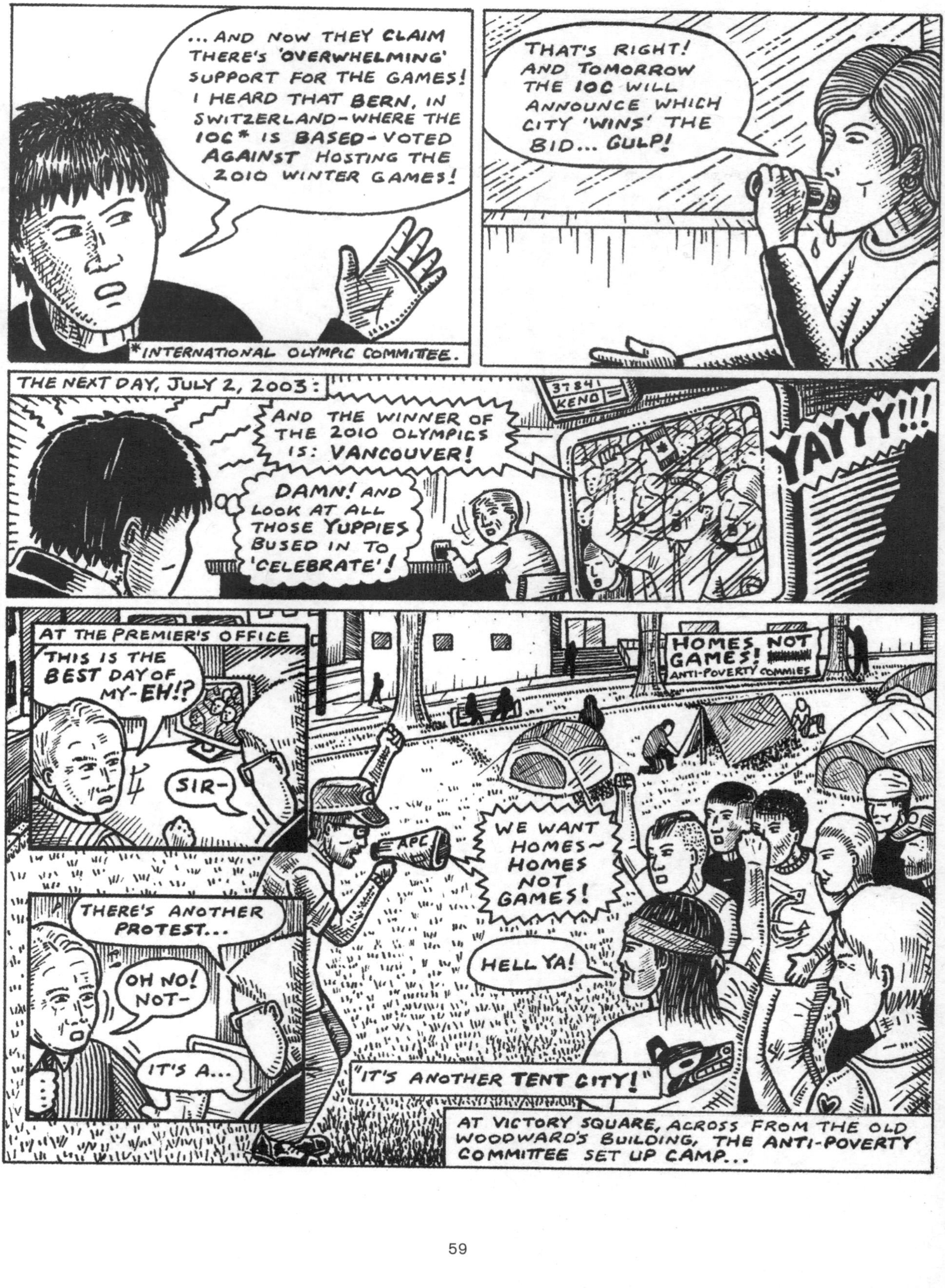
...AND NOW THEY CLAIM THERE'S 'OVERWHELMING' SUPPORT FOR THE GAMES! I HEARD THAT BERN, IN SWITZERLAND–WHERE THE IOC* IS BASED–VOTED AGAINST HOSTING THE 2010 WINTER GAMES!
*INTERNATIONAL OLYMPIC COMMITTEE.
THAT'S RIGHT! AND TOMORROW THE IOC WILL ANNOUNCE WHICH CITY 'WINS' THE BID... GULP!
THE NEXT DAY, JULY 2, 2003:
37841
KENO
AND THE WINNER OF THE 2010 OLYMPICS IS: VANCOUVER!
YAYYY!!!
DAMN! AND LOOK AT ALL THOSE YUPPIES BUSED IN TO 'CELEBRATE'!
AT THE PREMIER'S OFFICE
THIS IS THE BEST DAY OF MY–EH!?
SIR–
HOMES NOT GAMES!
ANTI-POVERTY COMMIES
APC
WE WANT HOMES~ HOMES NOT GAMES!
THERE'S ANOTHER PROTEST...
OH NO! NOT–
IT'S A...
HELL YA!
"IT'S ANOTHER TENT CITY!"
AT VICTORY SQUARE, ACROSS FROM THE OLD WOODWARD'S BUILDING, THE ANTI-POVERTY COMMITTEE SET UP CAMP...

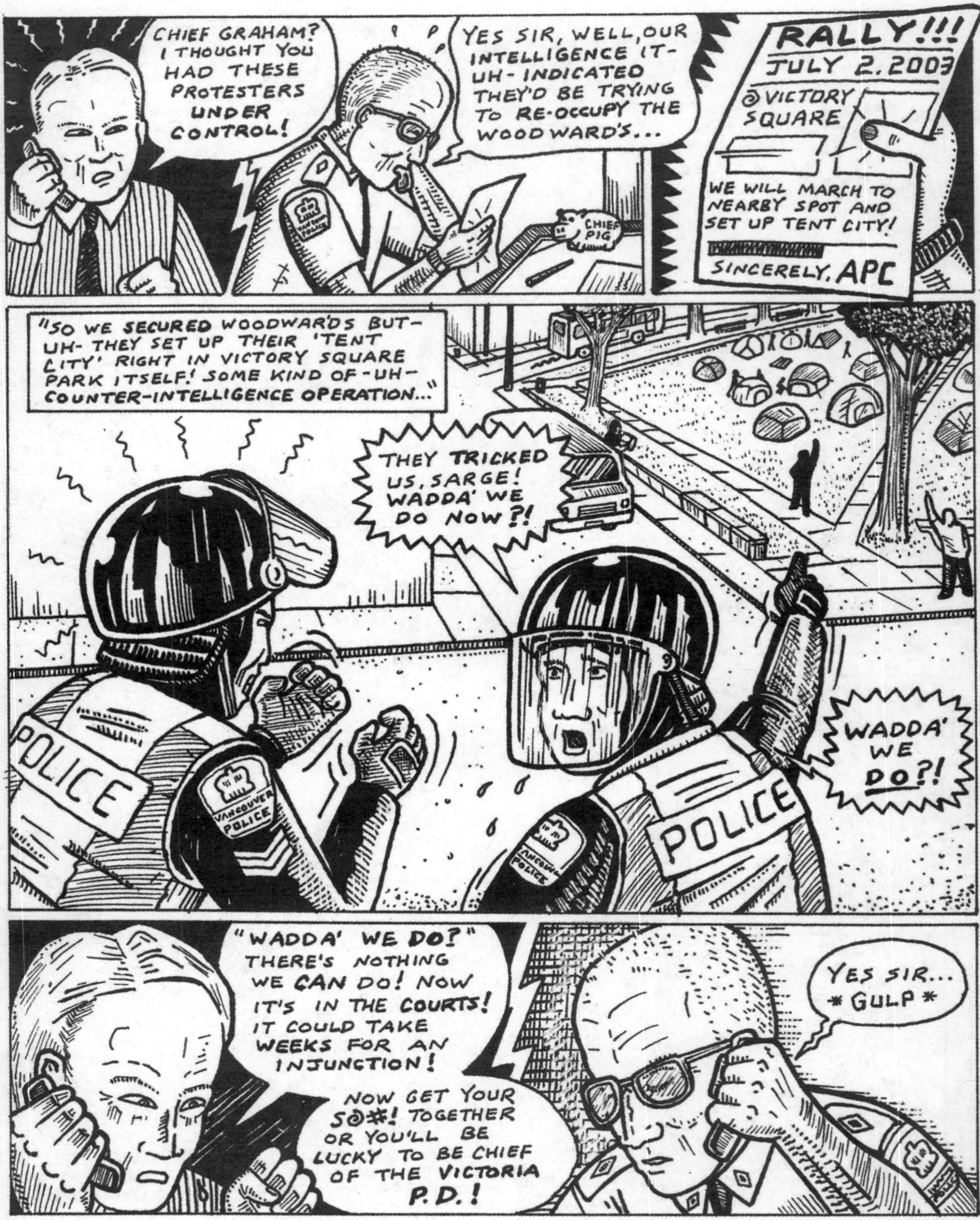
CHIEF GRAHAM? I THOUGHT YOU HAD THESE PROTESTERS UNDER CONTROL!
YES SIR, WELL, OUR INTELLIGENCE IT- UH- INDICATED THEY'D BE TRYING TO RE-OCCUPY THE WOODWARD'S...
CHIEF PIG
RALLY!!!
JULY 2, 2003
@ VICTORY SQUARE
WE WILL MARCH TO NEARBY SPOT AND SET UP TENT CITY!
SINCERELY, APC
"SO WE SECURED WOODWARD'S BUT- UH- THEY SET UP THEIR 'TENT CITY' RIGHT IN VICTORY SQUARE PARK ITSELF! SOME KIND OF -UH- COUNTER-INTELLIGENCE OPERATION..."
THEY TRICKED US, SARGE! WADDA' WE DO NOW?!
POLICE
VANCOUVER POLICE
WADDA' WE DO?!
POLICE
"WADDA' WE DO?" THERE'S NOTHING WE CAN DO! NOW IT'S IN THE COURTS! IT COULD TAKE WEEKS FOR AN INJUNCTION!
NOW GET YOUR S@#! TOGETHER OR YOU'LL BE LUCKY TO BE CHIEF OF THE VICTORIA P.D.!
YES SIR... *GULP*

TWO MONTHS LATER, THE CITY FINALLY GOT AN INJUNCTION AGAINST APC'S TENT CITY...

THEY MOVED TO ANOTHER PARK ON MAIN ST. FOR 2 MORE MONTHS.

THEN TO SCIENCE WORLD FOR ANOTHER MONTH, WHERE IT ENDED.

WITH VANCOUVER NOW CONFIRMED AS HOST CITY FOR THE 2010 OLYMPICS, MORE GROUPS CRITICAL OF THE GAMES EMERGED...

IMPACT ON COMMUNITIES COALITION

WE WANT COMMUNITY INPUT... MAYBE -OR- ACTUALLY...

WE WANT ACCOUNTA- BILITY!

2010 GAMES WATCH

OVER THE NEXT 3 YEARS, FORUMS AND SMALL PROTESTS OCCURRED, BUT FOR MANY THE IMPACTS WEREN'T YET OBVIOUS.

SAVE EAGLE RIDGE BLUFFS

GREENEST GAMES EVER?

THEN ON APRIL 17, 2006, A BLOCKADE WAS SET UP AT EAGLE RIDGE BLUFFS IN NORTH VANCOUVER.

THE BLUFFS WERE TO BE DESTROYED AS PART OF THE EXPANSION OF THE SEA-TO-SKY HIGHWAY LINKING VANCOUVER TO WHISTLER...

POLICE

WHISTLER, A SKI RESORT NORTH OF VAN- COUVER, WAS TO BE THE SITE OF SKI EVENTS. ON MAY 25, 2006, WEST VANCOUVER POLICE ARRESTED 24 OF THE PROTESTERS...

KIEWIT CONSTRU

1763 ROYAL PROCLAMATION

AMONG THOSE ARRESTED WAS 73-YEAR- OLD HARRIET NAHANEE, A PACHEEDAHT ELDER MARRIED INTO THE SQUAMISH.

ALSO ARRESTED WAS 78-YEAR-OLD BETTY KRAWCZYK, A WELL KNOWN LOCAL ENVIRONMENTAL ACTIVIST.

ON JUNE 15, 2006, HEAVY MACHINERY BELONGING TO VARIOUS CONSTRUCTION COMPANIES WORKING ON THE HIGHWAY EXPANSION WERE SABOTAGED.

DAMAGE: $50,000

MEANWHILE, IN THE DOWNTOWN EASTSIDE, HOMELESSNESS HAD DOUBLED FROM 2002...

BETWEEN 2002-2005, OVER 500 UNITS OF LOW-INCOME HOUSING WERE LOST DUE TO AN OLYMPIC REAL ESTATE 'BOOM'.

HOMES NOT GAMES

ON OCTOBER 23, 2006, APC SQUATTED THE EMPTY NORTH STAR HOTEL ON HASTINGS ST. SIX WERE ARRESTED THAT DAY...

THEN, ON OCT. 31, APC RALLIED AT CITY HALL WITH THE STATED INTENTION OF STORMING CITY COUNCIL CHAMBERS!

THEY'RE LEAVING! THEY TRICKED US-AGAIN!!

THE POLICE LOCKED DOWN CITY HALL, ONLY TO WATCH THE RALLY MARCH AWAY...

RICH GET RICHER POOR GET

WOMEN'S CITY HALL HOUSING TAKEOVER

A FEW BLOCKS ON, THEY OCCUPIED AN EMPTY BUILDING OWNED BY THE CITY. THE MAIN DEMAND WAS WOMEN'S HOUSING DUE TO A SURGE IN HOMELESS WOMEN.

JEEZ! ALL THIS 'HUBUB' ABOUT THE OLYMPICS... WHAT ARE THESE 'GAMES'?

VANCOUVER PUBLIC LIBRARY

I'M GONNA DO SOME STUDYING ON THE SUBJECT!

"ANCIENT GREEK RITUAL... 700 BC... NO SLAVES OR WOMEN ALLOWED..."

THAT'S NOT TOO INSPIRING.

"MODERN OLYMPICS: 1894... SET UP BY FRENCH BARON- PIERRE DE COUBERTIN..."

COLONIES ARE LIKE CHILDREN... VICTORY BY THE DOMINATED RACE NEED NOT BE SEEN AS A TEMPTATION TO REBEL, BUT CAN LEGITIMIZE COLONIAL RULE IN THE EYES OF THE 'WINNER'...

1932: BERLIN SELECTED HOST CITY FOR 1936 OLYMPICS. 1933: NAZIS TAKE POWER. JEWS AND ANTI-FASCISTS START A BOYCOTT..."

REPORTS OF NAZI TERROR AND TALK OF A BOYCOTT ARE ALL PART OF A JEWISH- COMMUNIST CONSPIRACY!

"AVERY BRUNDAGE, HEAD OF THE US OLYMPIC COMMITTEE, OPPOSED ANY BOYCOTT... HE WAS LATER IOC PRESIDENT, 1952 TO 1972."

"THE BRUTALITY OF THE NAZIS WAS WELL KNOWN AT THIS TIME. THE 1936 GAMES LEGITIMIZED AND STRENGTHENED THE NAZI REGIME AND ADOLF HITLER..."

"IT WAS THE NAZIS WHO INVENTED THE TORCH RELAY- AS A WAY TO PROMOTE FASCISM IN EUROPE. THEY SAW THE '36 GAMES AS A HUGE PROPAGANDA VICTORY..."

"1968 MEXICO CITY OLYMPICS: A MASS MOVEMENT OF STUDENTS AND WORKERS EMERGES, DEMANDING AN END TO STATE REPRESSION. HUNDREDS OF THOUSANDS JOIN RALLIES..."

"THEN, ON OCT. 2, TEN DAYS BEFORE THE GAMES, POLICE AND SOLDIERS OPEN FIRE, KILLING HUNDREDS. SEVERAL THOUSAND ARE BRUTALLY ARRESTED AND TORTURED..."

"THE IOC SAID NOTHING ABOUT THE MASSACRE, WHICH WAS COVERED UP BY THE GOVERNMENT..."

"BUT WHEN 2 BLACK AMERICAN ATHLETES DID BLACK POWER SALUTES, THE IOC STRIPPED THEIR MEDALS AND EJECTED THEM."

NAZIS... MASSACRES... WHAT KIND OF CLOWNS RUN THIS CIRCUS?

"JUAN ANTONIO SAMARANCH-IOC PRESIDENT FROM 1980 TO 2001. MEMBER OF FRANCO'S FASCIST REGIME IN SPAIN..."

"CORRUPTION..."

"THE BID PROCESS, IN WHICH CITIES BID FOR GAMES, LEADS TO WIDESPREAD BRIBERY OF IOC OFFICIALS... THIS WAS EXPOSED DURING THE 2000 SALT LAKE CITY GAMES."

"POLICE STATE..."

"THOUSANDS OF COPS AND SOLDIERS ARE USED FOR OLYMPIC SECURITY, COSTING HUNDREDS OF MILLIONS OF DOLLARS..."

"HOMELESSNESS..."

"CITIES, HOTEL AND PROPERTY OWNERS USE THE OLYMPICS FOR 'URBAN RENEWAL' ~ FORCING THE POOR OUT OF ENTIRE AREAS..."

"ECOLOGICAL DESTRUCTION..."

"NEW VENUES, ROADS, ETC., ALL REQUIRE VAST AMOUNTS OF CONCRETE, WITH GRAVEL TAKEN FROM RIVERS AND OTHER SITES..."

"CRIMINALIZATION..."

"POOR PEOPLE AND SOCIAL MOVEMENTS ARE TARGETED BY POLICE AND OFFICIALS AS THREATS TO PUBLIC IMAGE AND SECURITY..."

"PUBLIC DEBT..."

WE'RE GONNA NEED MORE!

"BILLIONS OF DOLLARS IN PUBLIC MONEY ARE PAID OUT TO CORPORATIONS FOR NEW VENUES, TRANSPORT, SECURITY, ETC...."

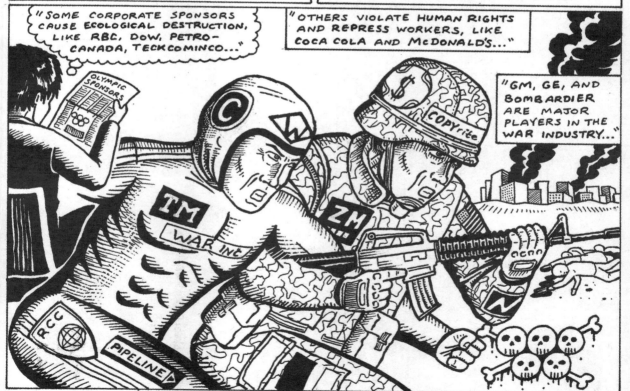

"SOME CORPORATE SPONSORS CAUSE ECOLOGICAL DESTRUCTION, LIKE RBC, DOW, PETRO-CANADA, TECKCOMINCO..."

"OTHERS VIOLATE HUMAN RIGHTS AND REPRESS WORKERS, LIKE COCA COLA AND McDONALD'S..."

"GM, GE, AND BOMBARDIER ARE MAJOR PLAYERS IN THE WAR INDUSTRY..."

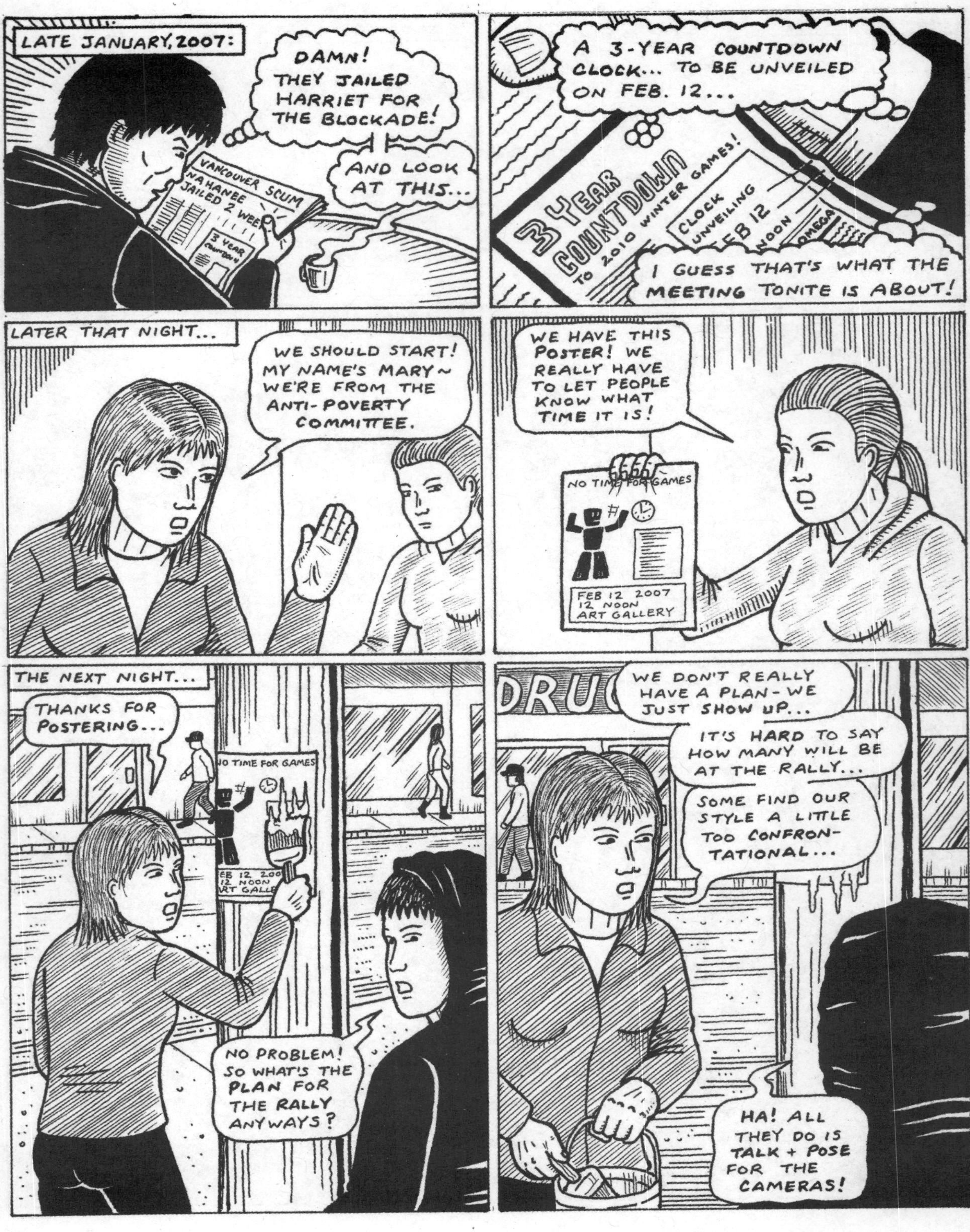
LATE JANUARY, 2007:
DAMN! THEY JAILED HARRIET FOR THE BLOCKADE!
AND LOOK AT THIS...
VANCOUVER SCUM
NAHANEE JAILED 2 WEE
3 YEAR COUNTDOWN
A 3-YEAR COUNTDOWN CLOCK... TO BE UNVEILED ON FEB. 12...
3 YEAR COUNTDOWN TO 2010 WINTER GAMES!
CLOCK UNVEILING FEB 12 NOON
OMEGA
I GUESS THAT'S WHAT THE MEETING TONITE IS ABOUT!
LATER THAT NIGHT...
WE SHOULD START! MY NAME'S MARY~ WE'RE FROM THE ANTI-POVERTY COMMITTEE.
WE HAVE THIS POSTER! WE REALLY HAVE TO LET PEOPLE KNOW WHAT TIME IT IS!
NO TIME FOR GAMES
FEB 12 2007 12 NOON ART GALLERY
THE NEXT NIGHT...
THANKS FOR POSTERING...
NO TIME FOR GAMES
NO PROBLEM! SO WHAT'S THE PLAN FOR THE RALLY ANYWAYS?
WE DON'T REALLY HAVE A PLAN- WE JUST SHOW UP...
IT'S HARD TO SAY HOW MANY WILL BE AT THE RALLY...
SOME FIND OUR STYLE A LITTLE TOO CONFRONTATIONAL...
HA! ALL THEY DO IS TALK + POSE FOR THE CAMERAS!

FEB. 12, 2007:

RESIST 2010

STOP THE CLOCK

COUNTDOWN TO DISASTER

AT 12 NOON, SOME 70 PROTESTERS SHOWED UP AT THE ART GALLERY— SITE OF THE CLOCK UNVEILING.

WHILE POLICE BLOCKED THE MOB, TWO SNUCK PAST THEIR LINE + STORMED THE STAGE JUST AS THE EVENT—BROADCAST ON LIVE TV—BEGAN.

FUCK 2010! FUCK YOUR CORPORATE CIRCUS!

AS THEY WERE ARRESTED, PANDEMONIUM BROKE OUT. EGGS + PAINT BOMBS WERE THROWN, WHILE POLICE VIOLENTLY ARRESTED FIVE MORE...

POLITICIANS + BUSINESSMEN ADDRESSED THE CROWD, BUT THEY HAD TO SHOUT OVER THE YELLING OF THE REMAINING PROTESTERS.

BOOO! HISSSS!

IT LOOKS LIKE YOUR TOMBSTONE!

10.96
05 22 57

OMEGA

LADIES + GENTLEMEN— THE OLYMPIC COUNTDOWN CLOCK!

THE OFFICIAL UNVEILING OF THE COUNTDOWN CLOCK WAS A DISASTER. IT ALSO SIGNALLED THE START OF A RADICAL ANT-OLYMPIC FIGHT.

THE NEXT NIGHT, AFTER THE LAST PRISONER WAS RELEASED...

OH MAN—DID WE SHUT 'EM DOWN!

OH HELL YA!

PUFF PUFF

YA—THAT WAS GREAT! BUT LISTEN—IN ONE MONTH THOSE OLYMPIC FOOLS ARE GONNA DO ANOTHER EVENT!

OUTSTANDING!

WHAT IS IT?

SOME KINDA FLAG-RAISING BULLSHIT AT CITY HALL!

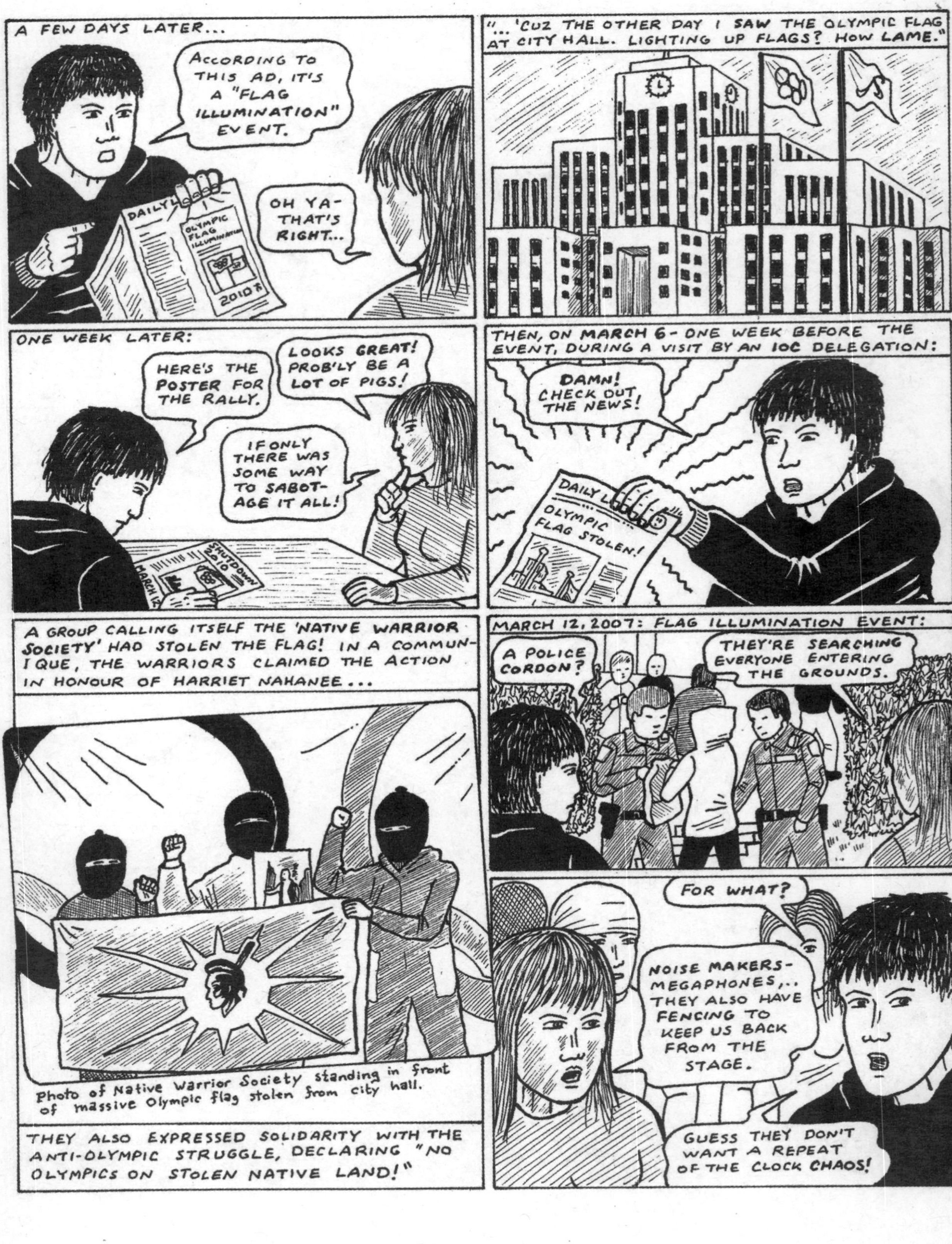
A FEW DAYS LATER...
ACCORDING TO THIS AD, IT'S A "FLAG ILLUMINATION" EVENT.
DAILY
OLYMPIC FLAG ILLUMINATION
2010
OH YA- THAT'S RIGHT...
"...'CUZ THE OTHER DAY I SAW THE OLYMPIC FLAG AT CITY HALL. LIGHTING UP FLAGS? HOW LAME."
ONE WEEK LATER:
HERE'S THE POSTER FOR THE RALLY.
LOOKS GREAT! PROB'LY BE A LOT OF PIGS!
IF ONLY THERE WAS SOME WAY TO SABOTAGE IT ALL!
SHUTDOWN 2010
MARCH 12
THEN, ON MARCH 6 - ONE WEEK BEFORE THE EVENT, DURING A VISIT BY AN IOC DELEGATION:
DAMN! CHECK OUT THE NEWS!
DAILY
OLYMPIC FLAG STOLEN!
A GROUP CALLING ITSELF THE 'NATIVE WARRIOR SOCIETY' HAD STOLEN THE FLAG! IN A COMMUNIQUE, THE WARRIORS CLAIMED THE ACTION IN HONOUR OF HARRIET NAHANEE...
Photo of Native Warrior Society standing in front of massive Olympic flag stolen from city hall.
THEY ALSO EXPRESSED SOLIDARITY WITH THE ANTI-OLYMPIC STRUGGLE, DECLARING "NO OLYMPICS ON STOLEN NATIVE LAND!"
MARCH 12, 2007: FLAG ILLUMINATION EVENT:
A POLICE CORDON?
THEY'RE SEARCHING EVERYONE ENTERING THE GROUNDS.
FOR WHAT?
NOISE MAKERS- MEGAPHONES,.. THEY ALSO HAVE FENCING TO KEEP US BACK FROM THE STAGE.
GUESS THEY DON'T WANT A REPEAT OF THE CLOCK CHAOS!

DESPITE 100 COPS - INCLUDING THE PUBLIC ORDER UNIT (IN SOFT HATS), HORSES, A HELICOPTER, ETC. - THE 200 PROTESTERS WERE ABLE TO DISRUPT THE EVENT WITH YELLING, WHISTLES, AND FOG HORNS.

SHUT 'EM DOWN!

HOMES NOT GAMES!!!

2010 HOMES NOT 2010 GAMES!

EARLIER THAT DAY THE OLYMPIC CLOCK HAD ALSO BEEN VANDALIZED IN PROTEST OF THE 10-MONTH JAIL SENTENCE HANDED TO BETTY KRAWCZYK.

FREE BETTY

THE 78-YEAR-OLD HAD BEEN JAILED FOR TAKING PART IN THE 2006 EAGLERIDGE BLUFFS BLOCKADE.

FROM THIS POINT ON, VANOC EVENTS WOULD HAVE LARGE POLICE DEPLOYMENTS, OR NOT BE PUBLICIZED.

...AND ANOTHER ONE BITES THE DUST!

DAILY
PROTESTERS DISRUPT FLAG CEREMONY

THE NEXT ANTI-OLYMPIC PROTEST WAS AT THE EAST VANCOUVER HQ OF VANOC, ON MAY 16/07.

Refuse to Retreat

ANTI-POVERTY COMMITTEE

ONCE AGAIN, THERE WERE DOZENS OF POLICE WITH FENCING ETC., BUT ONLY ABOUT 30 PROTESTERS FROM THE ANTI-POVERTY COMMITTEE...

AN APC SPEAKER ANNOUNCED THEIR NEW CAMPAIGN WOULD BE TO EVICT VANOC MEMBERS FROM THEIR HOMES + OFFICES

WE'RE GOING TO BRING THE CLASS WAR TO THEIR OFFICES AND THEIR DOORSTEPS!

3 DAYS LATER, HE WAS ARRESTED FOR "MAKING THREATS" BY COPS POSING AS JOURNALISTS...

HOW'ZABOUT WE DO AN INTERVIEW AT THE JAIL?

WHERE ARE THOSE FREAKIN' REPORTERS I WAS TO MEET?

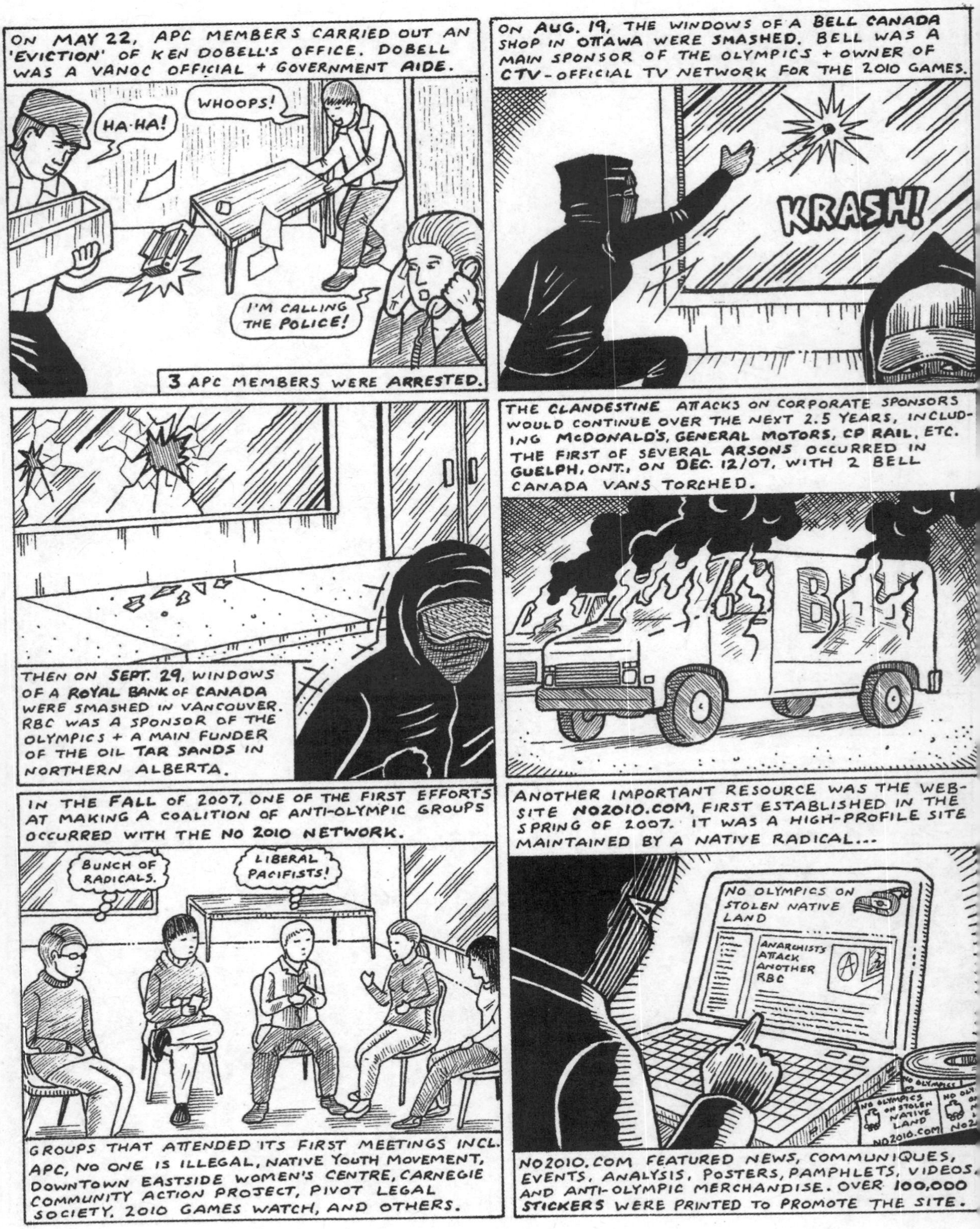
ON MAY 22, APC MEMBERS CARRIED OUT AN 'EVICTION' OF KEN DOBELL'S OFFICE. DOBELL WAS A VANOC OFFICIAL + GOVERNMENT AIDE.
HA-HA!
WHOOPS!
I'M CALLING THE POLICE!
3 APC MEMBERS WERE ARRESTED.
ON AUG. 19, THE WINDOWS OF A BELL CANADA SHOP IN OTTAWA WERE SMASHED. BELL WAS A MAIN SPONSOR OF THE OLYMPICS + OWNER OF CTV - OFFICIAL TV NETWORK FOR THE 2010 GAMES.
KRASH!
THEN ON SEPT. 29, WINDOWS OF A ROYAL BANK OF CANADA WERE SMASHED IN VANCOUVER. RBC WAS A SPONSOR OF THE OLYMPICS + A MAIN FUNDER OF THE OIL TAR SANDS IN NORTHERN ALBERTA.
THE CLANDESTINE ATTACKS ON CORPORATE SPONSORS WOULD CONTINUE OVER THE NEXT 2.5 YEARS, INCLUDING McDONALD'S, GENERAL MOTORS, CP RAIL, ETC. THE FIRST OF SEVERAL ARSONS OCCURRED IN GUELPH, ONT., ON DEC. 12/07, WITH 2 BELL CANADA VANS TORCHED.
IN THE FALL OF 2007, ONE OF THE FIRST EFFORTS AT MAKING A COALITION OF ANTI-OLYMPIC GROUPS OCCURRED WITH THE NO 2010 NETWORK.
BUNCH OF RADICALS.
LIBERAL PACIFISTS!
GROUPS THAT ATTENDED ITS FIRST MEETINGS INCL. APC, NO ONE IS ILLEGAL, NATIVE YOUTH MOVEMENT, DOWNTOWN EASTSIDE WOMEN'S CENTRE, CARNEGIE COMMUNITY ACTION PROJECT, PIVOT LEGAL SOCIETY, 2010 GAMES WATCH, AND OTHERS.
ANOTHER IMPORTANT RESOURCE WAS THE WEBSITE NO2010.COM, FIRST ESTABLISHED IN THE SPRING OF 2007. IT WAS A HIGH-PROFILE SITE MAINTAINED BY A NATIVE RADICAL...
NO OLYMPICS ON STOLEN NATIVE LAND
ANARCHISTS ATTACK ANOTHER RBC
NO OLYMPICS ON STOLEN NATIVE LAND
NO2010.COM
NO2010.COM FEATURED NEWS, COMMUNIQUES, EVENTS, ANALYSIS, POSTERS, PAMPHLETS, VIDEOS AND ANTI-OLYMPIC MERCHANDISE. OVER 100,000 STICKERS WERE PRINTED TO PROMOTE THE SITE.

IN THE FALL OF 2007, THE NATIONAL INDIGEN-OUS CONFERENCE OF MEXICO AND THE ZAPATISTA ARMY OF **NATIONAL LIBERATION (EZLN)** HOSTED AN INDIGENOUS GATHERING IN SONORA, MEXICO.

A DELEGATION OF NATIVES FROM BC ATTENDED AND RECEIVED A DECLARATION OF SUPPORT AGAINST THE 2010 OLYMPICS.

THE DECLARATION BECAME AN IMPORTANT DOCUMENT IN MOBILIZING ANTI-COLONIAL SOLIDARITY AGAINST THE OLYMPICS.

YA MAN—THE FREAKIN' ZAPATISTAS!

ZAPATISTA GATHERING ENDORSES ANTI-OLYMPIC MOVEMENT

ON FEB. 3, 2008, THE CARNEGIE COMMUNITY ACTION PROJECT HELD ITS FIRST ANNUAL **POVERTY OLYMPICS**, WITH SATIRICAL GAMES + MASCOTS.

END POVERTY

IT'S N

CREEPY THE COCKROACH   CHEWY THE RAT   ITCHY THE BEDBUG

A WEEK LATER, ON FEB.11/08, NO 2010 NETWORK AND **NATIVE 2010 RESISTANCE** RALLIED AGAINST A CORPORATE LUNCHEON MARKING THE 2-YEAR COUNTDOWN TO 2010. ABOUT 100 PEOPLE TOOK PART.

NATIVE RESISTANCE

BY THIS TIME, HOWEVER, THE NO 2010 NETWORK COLLAPSED. SOME GROUPS COULDN'T WORK TOGETHER AT THIS TIME...

YOUR GROUP SUCKS!

NO-YOUR GROUP SUCKS!!

BUT GROUPS CARRIED ON WITH THEIR OWN ACTIONS AGAINST THE OLYMPICS...

ON FEB.17/08, A SMALL APC RALLY **VANDALIZED** THE OLYMPIC CLOCK, WITH A PAINT-BOMB + POSTER GLUED ON ITS FRONT.

THE OLYMPICS ARE NOT WELCOME, YOU SELL-OUT!

?!

AFN AND FHFN OLYMPIC

ON FEB. 18, MEMBERS OF NATIVE 2010 RESISTANCE DISRUPTED A PRESS CONFERENCE OF THE ASSEMBLY OF FIRST NATIONS + THE FOUR HOST FIRST NATIONS PROMOTING THE GAMES. THEY DUMPED APPLES— RED ON THE OUTSIDE, WHITE ON THE INSIDE...

THE FOUR HOST FIRST NATIONS COMPRISED THE LOCAL INDIAN ACT BAND COUNCILS NEAR THE SITES OF OLYMPIC VENUES (VANCOUVER + WHISTLER).

CANADA WELCOMES THE WORLD

THEY WOULD RECIEVE MILLIONS OF DOLLARS IN EXCHANGE FOR THEIR COLLABORATION, WHILE BAND MEMBERS WOULD SEE LITTLE OF THIS.

NO OLYMPICS ON STOLEN NATIVE LAND

TO COUNTER THE IMAGE OF NATIVE SUPPORT FOR THE GAMES, ONE OF THE MAIN SLOGANS USED BY NATIVE RADICALS WAS 'NO OLYMPICS ON STOLEN NATIVE LAND'...

THIS SLOGAN EMPHASIZED THE THEFT OF NATIVE LAND IN THE PROVINCE AND ONGOING COLONIAL OCCUPATION...

HBC

IT ALSO CHALLENGED THE MYTH THAT RELATIONS BETWEEN CANADA + NATIVES WERE WITHOUT CONFLICT (INCL. THE HIGHEST RATES OF POVERTY, DISEASE, IMPRISONMENT, MISSING/ MURDERED WOMEN, HOMELESSNESS, ETC.).

HAHAHA!!

TO ROUND OUT THE 2008 'COUNTDOWN' EVENTS, ON FEB. 21, APC MEMBERS THREW PAINT ON THE WINDOWS OF THE BC PREMIER'S OFFICE.

AFTER THE DEMISE OF THE NO 2010 NETWORK AND, LATER, NATIVE 2010 RESISTANCE, A NEW COALITION WAS FORMED IN THE SPRING OF 2008.

HOW 'BOUT WE CALL IT 'OLYMPIC RESISTANCE NETWORK'?

'ORN AGAIN.

'ORN SUPREMACY.

'ORN IDENTITY.

ORN WOULD BE THE PRIMARY ANTI-OLYMPIC FORCE IN THE CITY. COMPRISED OF THE MORE RADICAL GROUPS, ORN PROMOTED ANTI-COLONIAL + ANTI-CAPITALIST ANALYSIS IN ITS WORK.

ORN HAD SEVERAL COMMITTEES, INCL. MEDIA, LOGISTICS, OUTREACH, LEGAL, AND MEDICAL.

...AND THAT'S HOW YOU SILKSCREEN.

I DON'T GET IT.

THEY HELD PUBLIC FORUMS, TRAINING SESSIONS, + CONFERENCES, AND PRODUCED NUMEROUS LEAFLETS, POSTERS, AND T-SHIRTS...

ORN ALSO PROMOTED THE 2010 CONVERGENCE, TO BE HELD FEB. 10-15 DURING THE GAMES.

CONVERGENCE FEB 2010

anti-colonial anti-capitalist

COAST SALISH TERRITORIES

www.No2010.Com

THE CONVERGENCE WAS FIRST ANNOUNCED AT THE INDIGENOUS GATHERING IN MEXICO, 2007.

BY THIS TIME (SPRING 2008), THE RCMP'S JOINT INTELLIGENCE GROUP (JIG) AND THE CANADIAN SECURITY INTELLIGENCE SERVICE (CSIS) HAD TARGETTED ORN MEMBERS.

TARGET HAS JUST ENTERED THE LOCATION, OVER...

WE'RE WITH THE JIG AND WE'D LIKE TO TALK TO YOU AB...

FUCK YOU, JIG PIG!

ALONG WITH A FEW INFILTRATORS INTO ORN, JIG + CSIS AGENTS VISITED ORGANIZERS AT THEIR HOMES + WORKPLACES, OR IN THE STREET.

IN RESPONSE, ORN HELD WORKSHOPS ON COUNTER-SURVEILLANCE + LEGAL RIGHTS WHEN DEALING WITH INTELLIGENCE AGENTS + COPS...

A STAKEOUT WILL COVER ALL ROUTES IN AND OUT OF THE AREA...

TARGET

TRIGGER

OP

DESPITE PROPAGANDA ABOUT POSSIBLE ISLAMIC 'TERROR' ATTACKS, INTELLIGENCE REPORTS SAW PROTESTS AS THE BIGGEST THREAT TO THE GAMES.

LEGITIMATE PROTESTERS DO NOT MAKE CARTOONS WITH OLYMPIC MASCOTS CARRYING MOLOTOVS!

Resist 2010

POLICE CONCERN OVER ANTI-OLYMPIC ACTIONS WAS NOT SIMPLY RHETORIC, HOWEVER, AS THE MILITANT CAMPAIGN AGAINST THE GAMES CONTINUED.

ONE OF THE MOST COMMON 'UNOFFICIAL' SLOGANS WAS 'RIOT 2010', LARGELY IN THE FORM OF GRAFFITI.

ON MAY 7/08, A TRUCK FROM KIEWIT - THE COMPANY EXPANDING HWY. 99 TO WHISTLER AND A MAJOR CONTRACTOR TO THE US MILITARY - WAS SET ON FIRE IN EAST VANCOUVER.

ON JUNE 24/08, MILITARY VEHICLES IN A DOWNTOWN VANCOUVER PARKADE WERE HIT WITH SEVERAL MOLOTOV COCKTAILS.

A COMMUNIQUE STATED "DESTROY THE MILITARY OLYMPIC POLICE STATE!"

THAT SAME NIGHT IN TORONTO, 14 VEHICLES AT A GENERAL MOTORS DEALERSHIP WERE TORCHED. A COMMUNIQUE CLAIMED THE ACTION AGAINST GM'S OLYMPIC SPONSORSHIP.

WHILE THE CAMPAIGN OF SABOTAGE + VANDALISM CONTINUED, ORN + OTHERS ACROSS THE COUNTRY BEGAN PREPARING FOR THE CP SPIRIT TRAIN.

JEEZ! NOT MUCH ACTION SINCE THOSE VANOC RATS WENT INTO HIDING!

WAIT - WHAT'S THIS? "CP 'SPIRIT TRAIN' TO PROMOTE OLYMPICS."

OH, REALLY?

YA - IT'S SUPPOSED TO CROSS THE COUNTRY FROM SEPT. TO OCT., "STOPPING IN SEVERAL CITIES."

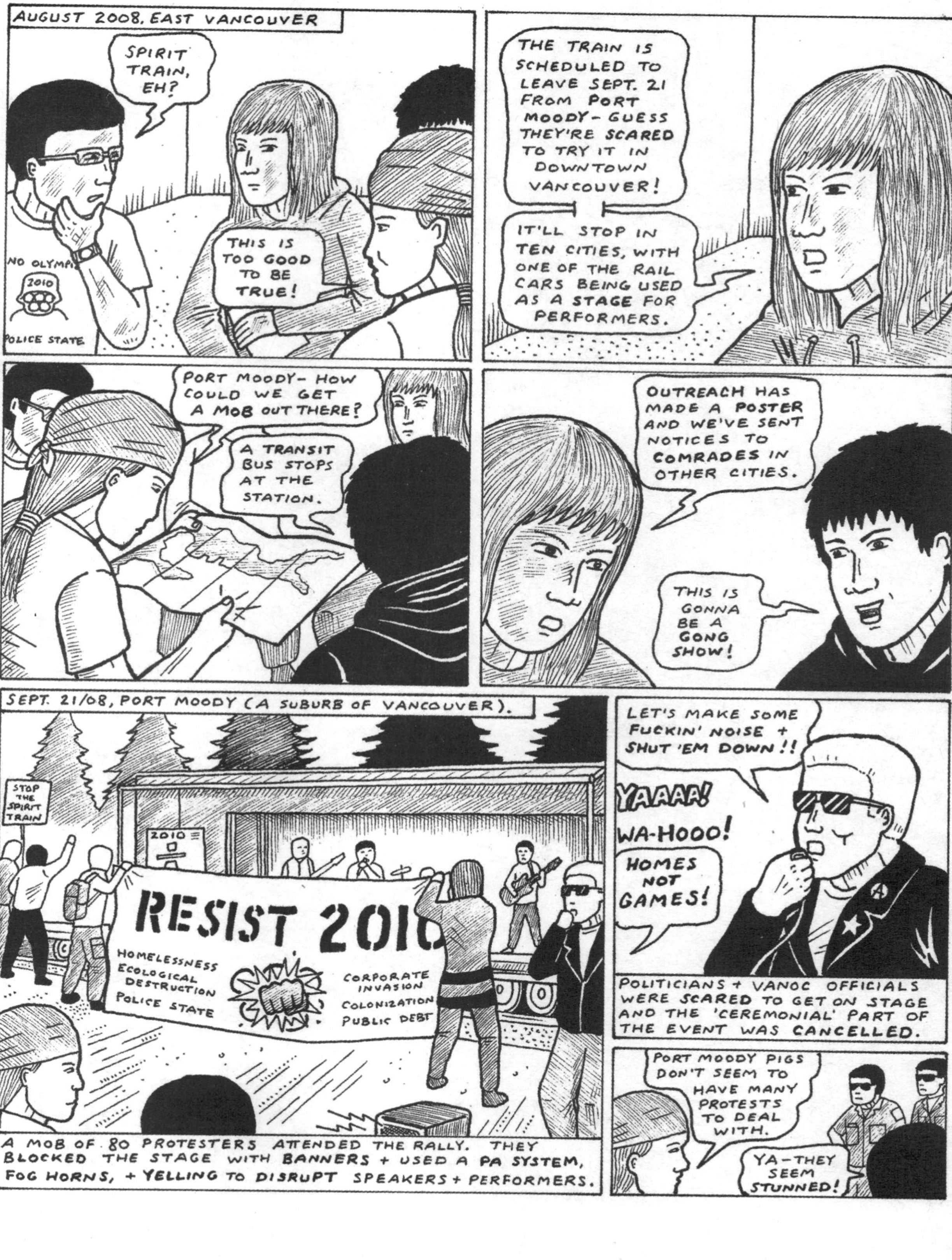
AUGUST 2008, EAST VANCOUVER
SPIRIT TRAIN, EH?
NO OLYMPICS 2010 POLICE STATE
THIS IS TOO GOOD TO BE TRUE!
THE TRAIN IS SCHEDULED TO LEAVE SEPT. 21 FROM PORT MOODY - GUESS THEY'RE SCARED TO TRY IT IN DOWNTOWN VANCOUVER!
IT'LL STOP IN TEN CITIES, WITH ONE OF THE RAIL CARS BEING USED AS A STAGE FOR PERFORMERS.
PORT MOODY- HOW COULD WE GET A MOB OUT THERE?
A TRANSIT BUS STOPS AT THE STATION.
OUTREACH HAS MADE A POSTER AND WE'VE SENT NOTICES TO COMRADES IN OTHER CITIES.
THIS IS GONNA BE A GONG SHOW!
SEPT. 21/08, PORT MOODY (A SUBURB OF VANCOUVER).
STOP THE SPIRIT TRAIN
2010
RESIST 2010
HOMELESSNESS
ECOLOGICAL DESTRUCTION
POLICE STATE
CORPORATE INVASION
COLONIZATION
PUBLIC DEBT
A MOB OF 80 PROTESTERS ATTENDED THE RALLY. THEY BLOCKED THE STAGE WITH BANNERS + USED A PA SYSTEM, FOG HORNS, + YELLING TO DISRUPT SPEAKERS + PERFORMERS.
LET'S MAKE SOME FUCKIN' NOISE + SHUT 'EM DOWN!!
YAAAA!
WA-HOOO!
HOMES NOT GAMES!
POLITICIANS + VANOC OFFICIALS WERE SCARED TO GET ON STAGE AND THE 'CEREMONIAL' PART OF THE EVENT WAS CANCELLED.
PORT MOODY PIGS DON'T SEEM TO HAVE MANY PROTESTS TO DEAL WITH.
YA-THEY SEEM STUNNED!

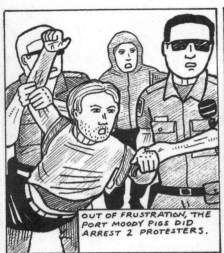

OUT OF FRUSTRATION, THE PORT MOODY PIGS DID ARREST 2 PROTESTERS.

IN EDMONTON, ANOTHER MOB OF PROTESTERS DISRUPTED THE SPIRIT TRAIN, WITH 2 CLIMBING ON IT TO DROP A BANNER BEFORE ESCAPING THE LARGE POLICE DEPLOYMENT.

Resist 2010

OUTSIDE TORONTO, A PROTESTER LOCKED DOWN ON THE TRAIN TRACKS + DELAYED THE TRAIN FOR HOURS.

NO OLYMPICS ON STOLEN NATIVE LAND. STOP 'SPIRIT THE TRAIN'

NO 2010

THE SPIRIT TRAIN WAS ALSO DISRUPTED IN WINNIPEG, MISSISSAUGA, + MONTREAL.

THE NEXT MAJOR EVENT FOR ORN WAS THE 1-YEAR COUNTDOWN IN FEB. 2009...

I PROPOSE A TORCH LIGHT MARCH!

TORCHES?

HMMM...

THE POLICE AND MILITARY ARE DOING A BIG TRAINING EXERCISE THEN...

THINK IT'LL BE COOL TO MARCH WITH TORCHES?

I DON'T THINK IT'LL BE A PROBLEM— THEY'RE ON THE DEFENSIVE RIGHT NOW WITH ALL THIS 'CIVIL LIBERTIES' STUFF.

YA— THEY'VE TAKEN HITS ON ALL THE SURVEILLANCE, BANNING OF SIGNAGE RELATED TO THE GAMES, THE 'SAFE ASSEMBLY' PROTEST PENS DURING THE GAMES... THEN THERE'S THE NEARLY #1 BILLION FOR SECURITY ITSELF...

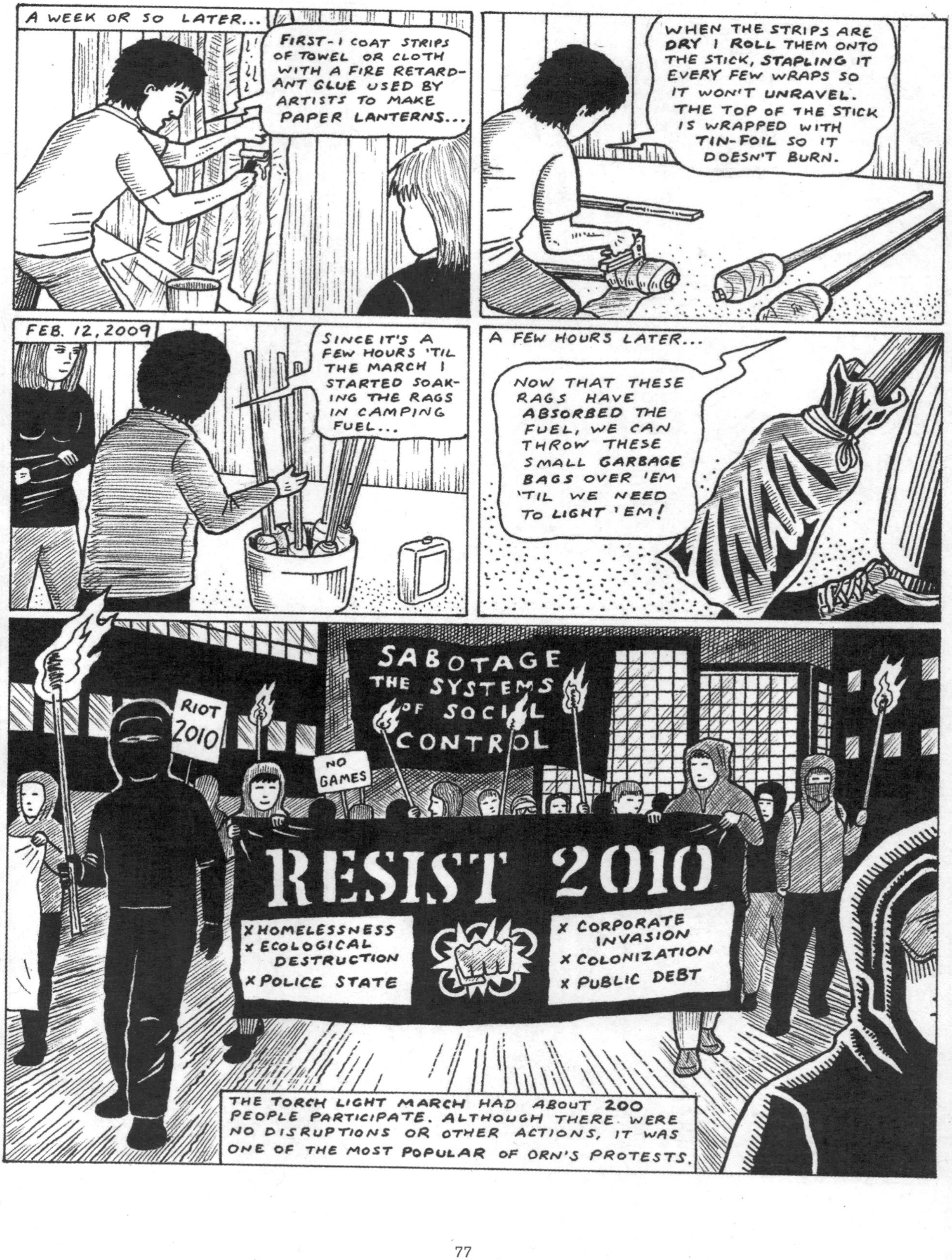

A WEEK OR SO LATER...
FIRST- I COAT STRIPS OF TOWEL OR CLOTH WITH A FIRE RETARD-ANT GLUE USED BY ARTISTS TO MAKE PAPER LANTERNS...
WHEN THE STRIPS ARE DRY I ROLL THEM ONTO THE STICK, STAPLING IT EVERY FEW WRAPS SO IT WON'T UNRAVEL. THE TOP OF THE STICK IS WRAPPED WITH TIN-FOIL SO IT DOESN'T BURN.
FEB. 12, 2009
SINCE IT'S A FEW HOURS 'TIL THE MARCH I STARTED SOAK-ING THE RAGS IN CAMPING FUEL...
A FEW HOURS LATER...
NOW THAT THESE RAGS HAVE ABSORBED THE FUEL, WE CAN THROW THESE SMALL GARBAGE BAGS OVER 'EM 'TIL WE NEED TO LIGHT 'EM!
SABOTAGE THE SYSTEMS OF SOCIAL CONTROL
RIOT 2010
NO GAMES
RESIST 2010
X HOMELESSNESS
X ECOLOGICAL DESTRUCTION
X POLICE STATE
X CORPORATE INVASION
X COLONIZATION
X PUBLIC DEBT
THE TORCH LIGHT MARCH HAD ABOUT 200 PEOPLE PARTICIPATE. ALTHOUGH THERE WERE NO DISRUPTIONS OR OTHER ACTIONS, IT WAS ONE OF THE MOST POPULAR OF ORN'S PROTESTS.

THE NEXT MAJOR EVENT WAS THE TORCH RELAY.

ALRIGHT-"THE OLYMPIC TORCH RELAY BEGINS OCT. 30 IN VICTORIA. IT'LL GO NORTH, CROSS THE COUNTRY, THEN HEAD BACK WEST FROM THE ATLANTIC COAST..."

THAT'S RIGHT, AND AS WE SAW WITH TURIN IN '06 AND CHINA IN '08, THE RELAY IS EXTREMELY VULNER-ABLE TO DISRUPTION. IN ITALY + FRANCE, PROTESTERS WERE ABLE TO EXTINGUISH IT SEVERAL TIMES!

THE RCMP WILL BE ESCORTING THE TORCH AND THERE WILL BE A LOT OF SECURITY!

OCT. 30, 2009, VICTORIA, BC: DESPITE 200 COPS, NEARLY 500 PROTESTERS CONDUCTED A 'ZOMBIE MARCH' FOR SEVEN HOURS IN THE RAIN AND SUCCEEDED IN BLOCKING THE TORCH, DELAYING IT, + DISRUPTING OFFICIAL CELEBRATIONS.

FUCK YOU AND YOUR FUCKIN' OLYMPICS!

IN THE FAR NORTH, THO' THERE WEREN'T ANY PROTESTS, THE TORCH WAS EXTINGUISHED SEVERAL TIMES BY COLD + WINDY WEATHER...

CRAP! IT'S GONE OUT AGAIN!

IT DOES LOOK LIKE A JOINT!

ONCE IT REACHED HALIFAX, PROTESTS BEGAN. IN TORONTO + MONTREAL, HUNDREDS WERE ABLE TO DISRUPT THE RELAY. IN KAHNAWAKE, THE RCMP WERE PROHIBITED FROM ENTERING.

IN GUELPH, ONT., PROTESTERS 'ACCIDENTLY' RAN INTO THE RELAY RUNNER, KNOCKING HER OVER. AT SIX NATIONS + ONEIDA, THE TORCH WAS BLOCKED FROM ENTRY TO THE REZ.

IN ALL, PROTESTS OCCURRED IN OVER 30 CITIES + TOWNS ACROSS THE COUNTRY.

IN VANCOUVER FEB. 12, 2010, THE TORCH WAS BLOCKED IN BOTH THE DOWNTOWN EASTSIDE + ON COMMERCIAL DR., WHERE ROCKS, STRING, AND BARBED WIRE WERE PLACED ACROSS THE STREET.

MEANWHILE, ON FEB. 10, THE ANTI-OLYMPIC CONVERGENCE HAD STARTED IN EAST VANCOUVER...

WELCOME TO TRADITIONAL COAST SALISH TERRITORY!

MEETINGS, WORKSHOPS, AND FORUMS WERE CONDUCTED WITH SOME 500 PARTICIPANTS.

SO IF YOU'RE JUST STOPPED RANDOMLY ON THE STREET BY POLICE YOU DON'T HAVE TO GIVE ID...

GROUPS CAME FROM ACROSS CANADA + THE US.

I WORKED WITH THE NO GAMES CHICAGO AND WE FOUGHT THE CITY'S BID FOR THE 2016 SUMMER GAMES...

A DELEGATION OF CIRCASSIANS ATTENDED, OPPOSED TO THE 2014 WINTER GAMES TO BE HELD IN SOCHI - THEIR TRADITIONAL LANDS.

IN THE 19TH CENTURY THE RUSSIANS COMMITTED GENOCIDE AGAINST OUR PEOPLE. WE OPPOSE ANY OLYMPICS IN SOCHI!

ON FEB. 12, THE DAY THE TORCH ARRIVED, THE OPENING CEREMONIES FOR THE OLYMPICS OCCURRED. A LARGE RALLY OF SOME 5,000 GATHERED AT THE ART GALLERY.

2010

WE'RE HERE TO TAKE BACK OUR CITY FROM THE OLYMPICS!!!

HOMES NOT GAMES

'TAKE BACK OUR CITY' WAS ORGANIZED BY THE 2010 WELCOMING COMMITTEE, INITIATED BY ORN WITH 50 COMMUNITY GROUPS.

ON STO[...]
NATIVE L[...]

RIOT 2010

NO ONE IS ILLEGAL

NATIVE ELDERS + WARRIORS, MOSTLY WOMEN, LED THE MARCH TO BC PLACE, SITE OF THE OPENING CEREMONIES.

AT BC PLACE, HUNDREDS OF COPS BLOCKED THE STREET + THREATENED THE ELDERS WITH VIOLENCE. A BLACK BLOC IN THE MARCH WAS ASKED TO MOVE TO THE FRONT LINE...

FUCK YOU PIG!!!

VANCOUV[...] POLI[...]

THE BLOC MADE SEVERAL CHARGES ON POLICE LINES, TAKING HATS, GLOVES, +FLASHLIGHTS. SEVERAL COPS WERE INJURED. DUE TO THE PROTEST, THE BC PREMIER + OTHER OFFICIALS WERE DELAYED, MISSING THE ANTHEM.

THE NEXT DAY, FEB. 13, WAS THE FIRST DAY OF THE GAMES. THE 2010 'HEART ATTACK' RALLY AIMED TO 'CLOG THE ARTERIES OF CAPITALISM'.

AMONG THE 400 PROTESTERS WAS A BLACK BLOC OF APPROXIMATELY 100 MILITANTS.

AS THE RALLY REACHED THE DOWNTOWN, MILITANTS SMASHED SEVERAL WINDOWS OF THE HUDSON'S BAY COMPANY, AN OLYMPIC SPONSOR + A PRIMARY AGENT IN THE COLONIZATION OF CANADA.

SMASH!

A TORONTO DOMINION BANK ALSO HAD WINDOWS SMASHED OUT...

AS THE MARCH HEADED TO THE WEST END, RIOT COPS WERE DEPLOYED...

THE BLACK BLOC USED A LADDER TO DETER COPS FROM ATTACKING THE REAR OF THE MARCH AS IT HEADED TO LION'S GATE BRIDGE.

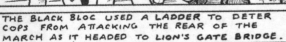

THE BRIDGE WAS A VITAL LINK TO VENUES IN WHISTLER; THE COPS SHUT DOWN THE BRIDGE FOR SEVERAL HOURS DUE TO THE PROTEST, DELAYING HUNDREDS OF OLYMPIC BUSES.

ON DENMAN ST. THE RIOT COPS ATTACKED, VIOLENTLY ARRESTING 7 PEOPLE, WHILE OTHERS ESCAPED THROUGH DE-ARRESTS.

THE NEXT DAY, SUNDAY FEB. 14, WAS THE 19TH ANNUAL WOMEN'S MARCH - A MEMORIAL FOR ALL MISSING + MURDERED WOMEN ACROSS THE COUNTRY.

ALTHO' THE MARCH WASN'T PART OF THE ANTI-OLYMPIC DAYS OF ACTION, ORN PROMOTED IT AS WELL.

SOME 5,000 PEOPLE PARTICIPATED IN THE MARCH, THE LARGEST EVER MEMORIAL RALLY.

FEB. 15 WAS FOCUSED ON HOUSING + HOMELESSNESS, ORGANIZED BY GROUPS IN THE DOWNTOWN EASTSIDE.

DURING A RALLY OF 250 PEOPLE, A MASSIVE BANNER WAS DROPPED FROM TELLIER TOWER ON HASTINGS STREET.

THEN AN EMPTY LOT AT 58 W. HASTINGS, OWNED BY CONCORD PACIFIC + LEASED TO VANOC FOR EXTRA PARKING, WAS OCCUPIED.

THE OLYMPIC TENT VILLAGE WOULD SHELTER SCORES OF HOMELESS, PROVIDING TENTS, FOOD, MEDICAL AID + SECURITY. IT WOULD LAST FOR 2 WEEKS AS A MAIN FOCUS OF OLYMPIC RESISTANCE.

THE ANTI-OLYMPIC CAMPAIGN SAW THE EMERGENCE (OR RENEWAL) OF A RADICAL, MILITANT, ANTI-COLONIAL + ANTI-CAPITALIST RESISTANCE MOVEMENT...

OVER SEVERAL YEARS, SOME 30 PUBLIC DIRECT ACTIONS + OVER 60 ATTACKS OCCURRED. OVER 100 PEOPLE WERE ARRESTED FROM 2006-10. THE CAMPAIGN RAISED PUBLIC AWARENESS ABOUT THE OLYMPIC INDUSTRY + ITS IMPACTS. IT ALSO HELPED DEFEND PEOPLE AGAINST THE WORST EFFECTS SUCH AS GREATER HOMELESSNESS + EROSION OF CIVIL LIBERTIES. IT WOULD ALSO INSPIRE + INFLUENCE THE UPCOMING G20 SUMMIT IN TORONTO...

ON THE FINAL DAY OF THE OLYMPICS - FEB. 28, A FINAL RALLY WAS HELD WHICH BLOCKED HASTINGS ST. FOR 7 HOURS AND ONLY ENDED AT 4:30AM WHEN RIOT COPS WERE USED TO CLEAR THE STREET.

RBC ARSON

AN INCENDIARY ANTI-COLONIAL + ANTI-CAPITALIST ACT.

AT AROUND 3:30AM ON MAY 18, 2010, TWO SHADOWY FIGURES ENTERED THE ATM AREA IN A ROYAL BANK OF CANADA BRANCH IN OTTAWA.

ONE POURED OUT A JUG OF GASOLINE WHILE THE OTHER THREW A MOLOTOV, IGNITING A FIREBALL.

FWOOSH!

THE FIRE RESULTED IN AN EST. #1.6 MILLION IN DAMAGES AND DESTROYED THE RBC BRANCH. THE ATTACK WAS VIDEO-TAPED BY THE MILITANTS AND USED IN A VIDEO COMMUNIQUE.

THE COMMUNIQUE CITED RBC'S FUNDING OF THE ALBERTA TAR SANDS + SPONSORSHIP OF THE OLYMPICS AS REASONS FOR THE ATTACK. THE GROUP, 'FFFC-OTTAWA', STATED THEY WOULD BE IN TORONTO FOR THE G20 AND ENDED: "WE SAY: THE FIRE THIS TIME."

THE ACTION WAS CONDEMN-ED BY REFORMISTS, COPS, + GOVERNMENT OFFICIALS. ALL WERE ESPECIALLY ALARMED BY THE GROUP'S REFERENCE TO THE TORONTO G20...

THIS IS DOMESTIC TERRORISM!

3 PEOPLE WERE LATER ARR-ESTED IN JUNE, ALTHO' ONLY 1 WAS CHARGED + CONVICTED.

ROGER CLEMENT, 58, WAS A RETIRED CIVIL SERVANT. IN DEC. 2010 HE WAS SENT-ENCED TO 3.5 YEARS IN PRISON FOR THE ARSON.

FIRE AND FLAMES

THE TORONTO G20 SUMMIT, JUNE 2010

IN JUNE 2010, SOUTHERN ONTARIO WAS THE SITE OF TWO MAJOR ECONOMIC SUMMITS: THE G8 ON JUNE 25 IN HUNTSVILLE AND THE G20 FROM JUNE 26-27 IN TORONTO.

○ HUNTSVILLE

OTTAWA ○
⊙
MONTREAL

TORONTO ●

LAKE ONTARIO

○ 50 100 150 KM

THE G20 BEGAN IN 1999, COMPRISED OF THE G8 PLUS THE NEXT 12 LARGEST ECONOMIES: CHINA, INDIA, SAUDI ARABIA, MEXICO, BRAZIL, S. KOREA, ARGENTINA, AUSTRALIA, INDONESIA, S. AFRICA, TURKEY, PLUS THE EUROPEAN UNION.

'G20 TORONTO

THE PITTSBURGH G20, HELD IN SEPT. 2009, ALSO SAW SIGNIFICANT CLASHES, PROPERTY DAMAGE, + THE USE OF AN LRAD (LONG-RANGE ACOUSTIC DEVICE) AGAINST PROTESTERS.

THE G8 BEGAN IN 1997 COMPRISED OF THE TOP 8 INDUSTRIALIZED STATES: BRITAIN, CANADA, FRANCE, GERMANY, ITALY, JAPAN, RUSSIA, AND THE U.S. WITH RUSSIA, THE G8 REPLACED THE G7.

BECAUSE THE G8 DICTATED GLOBAL ECONOMICS, ITS SUMMITS WERE THE FOCUS OF MASS PROTESTS, INCL. GENOA IN 2001 + ROSTOCK, GERMANY, 2007.

IN APRIL 2009, THE G20 SUMMIT IN LONDON SAW TENS OF THOUSANDS OF PROTESTERS IN THE STREET + A MASSIVE POLICE OPERATION.

POLICE ATTACKS ON 'NON-VIOLENT' PROTESTERS RESULTED IN ONE DEATH - IAN TOMLINSON - A LOCAL RESIDENT BEATEN BY POLICE.

IN THE FALL OF 2009 IT WAS ANNOUNCED THAT, ALONG WITH THE G8 IN HUNTSVILLE, THE G20 WOULD MEET IN TORONTO.

G20 IN TORONTO? THIS IS GONNA BE AWESOME!

TORONTO SCUM
G20 TO BE IN TORONTO

THIS ANNOUNCEMENT ACCELERATED LOCAL ORGANIZING, WHICH HAD BEEN FOCUSED ON THE G8 IN HUNTSVILLE, A SMALL RURAL TOWN.

LIKE PRIOR SUMMITS, GROUPS IN TORONTO BEGAN A LARGE MOBILIZING CAMPAIGN: EDUCATIONAL MATERIALS, SPEAKING TOURS, LOGISTICS, ETC.

THE TORONTO COMMUNITY MOBILIZATION NETWORK (TCMN) WAS ESTABLISHED TO COORDINATE THE EFFORTS OF MANY DIVERSE GROUPS.

IN OTTAWA + MONTREAL - WHERE THE ANTI-CAPITALIST CONVERGENCE OF 2001 HAD BEEN RESURRECTED - RADICALS ALSO BEGAN ORGANIZING TO BRING CARAVANS TO TORONTO.

THE TCMN WORKED WITH THESE GROUPS AND ALSO COMMUNICATED WITH NGO'S AND UNIONS TO COORDINATE ACTIONS DURING THE PROTESTS.

TCMN INCL. NO ONE IS ILLEGAL, ONTARIO COALITION AGAINST POVERTY (OCAP), + OTHERS.

THE MOST MILITANT WAS THE SOUTHERN ONTARIO ANARCHIST RESISTANCE (SOAR), BASED IN SMALLER CITIES OUTSIDE OF TORONTO.

AS JUNE NEARED, THE OVERALL PLAN WAS FOR A "PEOPLE'S SUMMIT" JUNE 18-20, THEMED DAYS OF RESISTANCE JUNE 21-24, AND 3 DAYS OF ACTION, FROM JUNE 25-27...

THE MOST MILITANT ACTIONS PROPOSED WERE SOAR'S "GET OFF THE FENCE" MARCH ON JUNE 26 AND "SATURDAY NIGHT FEVER" THAT EVENING.

PEOPLE'S SUMMIT, JUNE 19:

HEY BRO'~ VANCOUVER, RIGHT? HOW YOU FEELIN' THE SUMMIT?

YA-HEY... ACTUALLY, I'M GETTING WORRIED!

IT'S DOMINATED BY NGO'S + REFORMISTS! THAT GREENPEACER WAS DENOUNCING MILITANTS IN HIS 'DIRECT ACTION' CLASS - OUR ONLY HOPE ARE THE QUEBECOIS!

I HEAR YA, BRO'.

THERE'S STILL SOME GOOD PEEPS HERE. BUT YO-CHECK THIS OUT: SOAR. LOTS OF COMRADES IN ALL THE NEARBY CITIES!

THAT'LL BE $2.99, DAWG.

SOUTHERN ONTARIO ANARCHIST RESISTANCE

YA- I GOT ONE OF THOSE FROM THE FREE TABLE...

I HAVEN'T HAD A CHANCE TO CHECK IT OUT- BUT I WILL!

SOAR... LIKE AN EAGLE!

THE FIRST DAY OF RESISTANCE, JUNE 21, WAS A GENERAL CALL-OUT TO "DEFEND THE RIGHTS OF ALL." IT WAS A HOT DAY, AS IT WOULD BE ALL WEEK.

DAMN! THESE BIKE PIGS ARE POWER TRIPPIN'!

YA, REAL JERK-OFFS!

ABOUT 100 PEOPLE RALLIED IN A DOWNTOWN PARK, ALONG WITH AN EQUAL NUMBER OF COPS WHO SURROUNDED IT + PROHIBITED FLAG + BANNER POLES. THEY AT FIRST BLOCKED THE RALLY FROM LEAVING THE PARK, THEN ENCIRCLED IT WITH BICYCLE COPS AS IT MARCHED.

JUNE 22, A TUESDAY, WAS THEMED "QUEERING THE G20," A RALLY FOR 'GENDER JUSTICE, QUEER, + DISABILITY RIGHTS' WITH 200 PEOPLE.

POLICE STATE OUT OF OUR COMMUNITIES

LOVE IS NOT A CRIME!

GENDER JUSTICE NOW!

GAY AS F@XK

BY THIS TIME, DOWNTOWN TORONTO WAS OCCUPIED BY AN ARMY OF COPS, POSITIONED AT INTERSECTIONS, OUTSIDE BANKS, ETC.

THIS WAS PART OF THE LARGEST SECURITY OPERATION IN CANADIAN HISTORY. IT INCLUDED 6 KM OF FENCING AROUND THE G20 SITE.

MUCH OF THE $1 BILLION SPENT PAID FOR SOME 10,000 COPS, 4,000 MILITARY TROOPS, AND 5,000 SECURITY GUARDS (SOME 19,000 TOTAL).

THE THEME FOR WED. JUNE 23 WAS "CLIMATE + ENVIRONMENTAL JUSTICE," LARGELY ECO-NGO'S SUCH AS THE RAINFOREST ACTION NETWORK.

THE MAIN FOCUS WAS THE ALBERTA TAR SANDS, WITH ABOUT 500 PEOPLE PARTICIPATING. AGAIN THERE WAS A LARGE + AGGRESSIVE COP PRESENCE.

JUNE 24 WAS THE INDIGENOUS PEOPLE'S RALLY, ORGANIZED BY DEFENDERS OF THE LAND, NATIVE COUNCIL FIRE, AND OTHERS.

WITH 1,000 PEOPLE IT WAS THE LARGEST RALLY BUT WITH LITTLE POLICE HARASSMENT AS ORGANIZERS COLLABORATED WITH THE POLICE.

THE NEXT DAY, FRI. JUNE 24, WAS THE FIRST DAY OF ACTION: 'JUSTICE FOR OUR COMMUNITIES!' ORGANIZED BY OCAP, IT SAW SOME 5,000 PEOPLE MARCH.

THE MARCH SAW THE FIRST SKIRMISHES WITH POLICE, STARTING WITH THE VIOLENT ARREST OF A DEAF MAN BY BIKE COPS...

AS THE MARCH TRIED TO MOVE TOWARDS THE G20 MEETING SITE IT WAS BLOCKED AT EVERY TURN BY RIOT COPS, INCL. HORSES.

IN THE EARLY MORNING HOURS OF JUNE 25, COPS RAIDED SEVERAL HOMES + ARRESTED SOME OF THE SOAR ORGANIZERS STAYING IN TORONTO.

WAKE UP YOU ASSHOLES! SHOW ME YOUR HANDS! NOW!

HUH? WHA..?

AT 1 PM, THE 'OFFICIAL' LABOUR + NGO RALLY BEGAN, WITH ABOUT 12,000 PEOPLE GATHERING IN HEAVY RAIN AT QUEEN'S PARK.

ABOLISH CAPITALISM

BRING THE TROOPS HOME NOW! CANADA OUT OF AFGHAN

THE 'PEOPLE FIRST' RALLY MARCHED A FEW BLOCKS (TO QUEEN + SPADINA) THEN TURNED BACK TO THE PARK.

NOTHIN' TO SEE HERE - KEEP MOVING!

THIS WAS ALSO THE START OF SOAR'S 'GET OFF THE FENCE', A BREAK-AWAY MARCH INTENDED TO GO TO THE SECURITY FENCE + CONFRONT THE G20.

FUCK THE POLICE!

GET BACK!

THIS MARCH WAS COMPRISED OF ABOUT 1,000 MILITANTS. IT WAS AT FIRST BLOCKED BY THE UNION MARSHALS + THEN BY THE RIOT COPS.

AS A BLACK BLOC CONSOLIDATED ITSELF, THE MARCH REVERSED DIRECTION, CATCHING THE COPS FOLLOWING IN THE REAR OFF-GUARD...

SMASH!

KRASH

TO SERVE & PROTECT

POLICE

MOST OF THESE COPS FLED, ABANDONING SEVERAL VEHICLES, WHICH WERE SMASHED UP. ONE COP WAS TRAPPED IN HIS CAR AS IT WAS TRASHED.

THEN ONE OF THE ABANDONED COP CARS WAS SET ON FIRE AS SPECTATORS CHEERED...

THE MARCH CONTINUED EAST ON QUEEN STREET, SMASHING CORPORATE WINDOWS AS IT MOVED.

AT BAY ST. THE MARCH TURNED SOUTH. AT KING ST. MILITANTS TRIED TO BREAK A WINDOW AT A BANK OF MONTREAL, WITH LITTLE EFFECT...

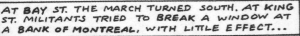

UNTIL A THROWN HAMMER STUCK INTO THE GLASS, SHATTERING IT...

ANOTHER MILITANT RAN UP TO THE WINDOW + RETRIEVED THE HAMMER.

AT BAY + KING STREETS, POLICE WERE AGAIN CAUGHT OFF GUARD + ABANDONED MORE OF THEIR VEHICLES, WHICH WERE THEN ATTACKED.

WITHIN MINUTES, TWO MORE COP CARS WERE BURNING, SPEWING THICK BLACK SMOKE INTO THE DOWNTOWN FINANCIAL DISTRICT...

HERE THE MOB HESITATED, SEEMINGLY MESMERIZED BY THE BURNING COP CARS.

LET'S GO! WE'RE JUST A BLOCK FROM THE FENCE!

OH YA— THE FENCE!

BUT THEN A PLATOON OF RIOT COPS MOVED IN TO BLOCK THE FENCE.

OH SHIT!

RIOT PIGS!

AS THE CROWD TURNED TO MOVE BACK DOWN BAY ST., MORE RIOT COPS MOVED TO BLOCK THE WAY.

POLICE   POLICE   POL

BLOCKED TO THE NORTH + SOUTH, THE MARCH TURNED EAST, TOWARDS YONGE STREET, A MAJOR COMMERCIAL DISTRICT...

NOW THE MOST EXTENSIVE PROPERTY DAMAGE WOULD OCCUR. AN AMERICAN APPAREL STORE HAD ITS WINDOWS SMASHED. MANNEQUINS WERE LOOTED, DISMEMBERED, AND BODY PARTS USED TO BREAK WINDOWS OF OTHER STORES.

ANY PIECE OF CONSTRUCTION, LOOSE CONCRETE, STICKS, + EVEN GOLF BALLS WERE USED TO DAMAGE CORPORATE PROPERTY...

SMASH!

KRASH!

CLUNK

ENOUGH WITH THE GOLF BALLS!

STOP THROWING THE GOLF BALLS!

THE GOLF BALLS WERE DISCOURAGED AS THEY DIDN'T BREAK ANYTHING BUT INSTEAD RICOCHETED WILDLY IN THE STREET.

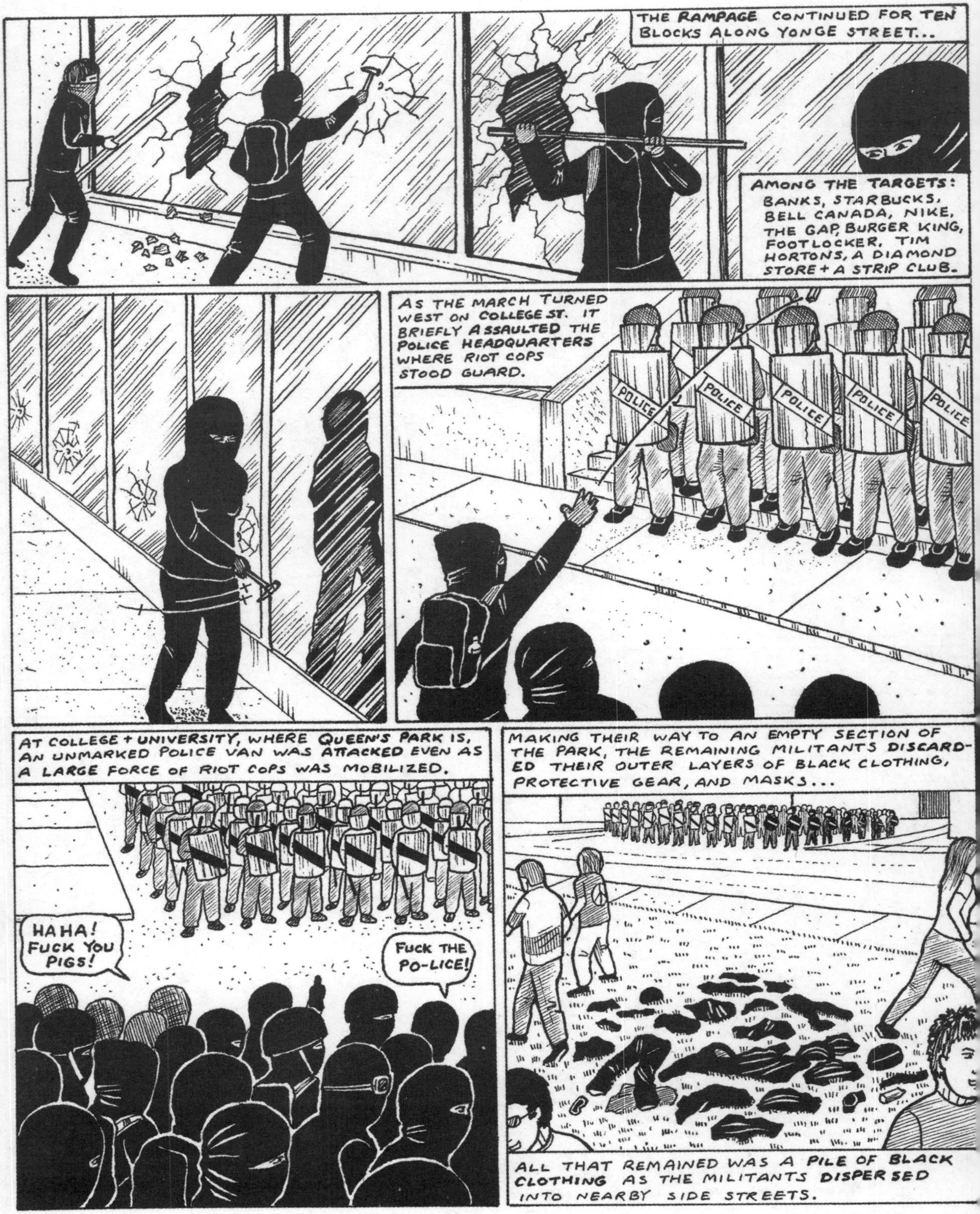
THE RAMPAGE CONTINUED FOR TEN BLOCKS ALONG YONGE STREET...
AMONG THE TARGETS: BANKS, STARBUCKS, BELL CANADA, NIKE, THE GAP, BURGER KING, FOOTLOCKER, TIM HORTONS, A DIAMOND STORE + A STRIP CLUB.
AS THE MARCH TURNED WEST ON COLLEGE ST. IT BRIEFLY ASSAULTED THE POLICE HEADQUARTERS WHERE RIOT COPS STOOD GUARD.
POLICE
POLICE
POLICE
POLICE
POLICE
AT COLLEGE + UNIVERSITY, WHERE QUEEN'S PARK IS, AN UNMARKED POLICE VAN WAS ATTACKED EVEN AS A LARGE FORCE OF RIOT COPS WAS MOBILIZED.
HAHA! FUCK YOU PIGS!
FUCK THE PO-LICE!
MAKING THEIR WAY TO AN EMPTY SECTION OF THE PARK, THE REMAINING MILITANTS DISCARD-ED THEIR OUTER LAYERS OF BLACK CLOTHING, PROTECTIVE GEAR, AND MASKS...
ALL THAT REMAINED WAS A PILE OF BLACK CLOTHING AS THE MILITANTS DISPERSED INTO NEARBY SIDE STREETS.

A LARGE GROUP OF BIKE + FOOT COPS ENTERED THE PARK FROM THE SOUTH + *ATTACKED PACIFIST* PROTESTERS THAT REMAINED AFTER THE 'PEOPLE FIRST' RALLY.

MEANWHILE, AT QUEEN + SPADINA, A LARGE CROWD OF ONLOOKERS HAD GATHERED TO WATCH THE FIRST TORCHED COP CAR, STILL SMOLDERING...

HERE, A PLATOON OF ONTARIO PROVINCIAL POLICE MARCHED IN, ESCORTING FIRE FIGHTERS. THEIR CONDUCT ANTAGONIZED THE CROWD...

THEN ANOTHER ABANDONED COP CAR WAS SET ON FIRE - THE FOURTH ONE OF THE DAY...

MORE RIOT COPS WERE SENT IN, INCL. RCMP + NEWFOUNDLAND COPS. HORSES WERE USED TO CHARGE INTO THE CROWD + CATCH 'AGITATORS'.

A SMALL GROUP OF PACIFIST PROTESTERS SAT IN THE STREET + ENCOURAGED THE CROWD TO SING 'OH CANADA', THE NATIONAL ANTHEM.

AS SOON AS THEY FINISHED, THE COPS CHARGED.

FOR THE REST OF THE EVENING THE COPS RAMPAGED THRU' THE STREETS, ASSAULTING PACIFIST PROTESTERS + CITIZENS...

THEIR CAMPAIGN OF REVENGE, FUELED BY THEIR HUMILIATION AT HAVING LOST CONTROL OF THE STREETS, CONTINUED INTO THE NEXT DAY.

AT 5AM ON JUNE 27, COPS RAIDED A UNIVERSITY BUILDING WHERE PROTESTERS FROM QUEBEC WERE STAYING.

THEY ARRESTED 50, CLAIMING TO HAVE FOUND BLACK CLOTHING, BRICKS, + ROCKS...

AT AN AFTERNOON JAIL SOLIDARITY RALLY COPS AGAIN ATTACKED PROTESTERS + ARRESTED MORE.

AN UNMARKED POLICE VAN WAS USED TO SNATCH A PRISONER FROM THE CROWD...

AT 6PM, AT QUEEN + SPADINA, RIOT COPS SURROUNDED A CROWD OF 200 AND HELD THEM IN A 'KETTLE' FOR HOURS IN HEAVY RAIN.

AFTER SEVERAL HOURS THE CROWD WAS ARRESTED. IT INCLUDED PROTESTERS, CITIZENS, + REPORTERS.

A TOTAL OF 1150 PEOPLE WERE ARRESTED JUNE 26-27, THE LARGEST MASS ARRESTS IN CANADIAN HISTORY.

AN OLD MOVIE STUDIO WAS USED AS A JAIL. PRISONERS WERE HELD IN CAGES + MANY REPORTED ABUSIVE CONDITIONS. SOME WERE ZIP-TIED FOR UP TO TEN HOURS.

EVENTUALLY, CONSPIRACY CHARGES WERE LAID AGAINST 17 PEOPLE, MOSTLY ORGANIZERS WITH SOAR + CLAC. THE CASE WAS BASED ON TWO COP INFILTRATORS: BRENDA CAREY + BINDO SHOWAN.

ALTOGETHER, 17 LONG-TERM UNDERCOVER COPS INFILTRATED A WIDE VARIETY OF GROUPS FOR AT LEAST 1.5 YEARS PRIOR TO THE G20, INCL. GREENPEACE, COUNCIL OF CANADIANS, TCMN, AND OTHERS.

IN NOV. 2011, SIX OF THE CONSPIRACY DEFENDANTS PLED GUILTY IN A PLEA BARGAIN TO COUNSELLING MISCHIEF OVER $5000. IN EXCHANGE, CONSPIRACY CHARGES WERE DROPPED. THE SIX WERE SENTENCED TO JAIL TERMS OF 6-24 MONTHS. OTHER MILITANTS RECIEVED SIMILAR SENTENCES.

DESPITE THE REPRESSION AND MASSIVE SECURITY OPERATION, THE TORONTO G20 WAS ONE OF THE MOST MILITANT MANIFESTATIONS OF ANTI-CAPITALIST RESISTANCE IN RECENT HISTORY (IN NORTH AMERICA).

THE OCCUPY MOVEMENT

STOP CORPORATE GREED!

IN SEPT. 2011, PROTESTERS SET UP A TENT CITY IN NEW YORK CITY'S WALL ST. DISTRICT, A HUB OF US + GLOBAL FINANCIAL CAPITAL.

HEEDING A CALL FROM VANCOUVER-BASED 'ADBUSTERS', OCCUPY WALL ST. TARGETED CORPORATE GREED + ECONOMIC INEQUALITY.

"None are more hopelessly enslaved than those who falsely believe they are free." -Goethe.

WE ARE THE 99%

THE MOVEMENT WAS INSPIRED BY THE 'ARAB SPRING'~REVOLTS IN N. AFRICA + THE MIDDLE EAST. UPRISINGS IN TUNISIA + EGYPT FORCED DICTATORS OUT OF POWER.

THE REVOLTS IN TUNISIA + EGYPT WERE BASED IN OCCUPATIONS OF CITY PLAZAS. WHITE-WASHED AS 'NON-VIOLENT', THE REBELLIONS SAW WIDESPREAD CLASHES WITH POLICE THAT KILLED HUNDREDS—INCLUDING POLICE. STATE BUILDINGS WERE ALSO LOOTED + BURNED.

AFTER OCCUPYING ZUCCOTTI PARK IN NEW YORK FOR 2 WEEKS, SOME 700 WERE ARRESTED ON OCT. 1 DURING A MARCH ON THE BROOKLYN BRIDGE.

A CALL WENT OUT FOR A GLOBAL DAY OF SOLIDARITY TO BE HELD ON OCT. 15.

NICE DAY FOR A REVOLUTION

IN OVER A THOUSAND CITIES + TOWNS, RALLIES WERE HELD WITH HUNDREDS OF TENT CITIES ESTABLISHED. THOUSANDS OF PEOPLE JOINED IN.

THE OCCUPY SITES SET UP FOOD KITCHENS, MEDIA COMMITTEES, LIBRARIES, CLINICS, ETC. AS AUTONOMOUS, SELF-ORGANIZED CAMPS.

GENERAL ASSEMBLIES WERE HELD DAILY TO DECIDE ON CAMP ORGANIZATION, TASKS, ETC.

THE ASSEMBLIES + CONCENSUS MODELS WERE ADOPTED FROM TENT OCCUPATIONS THAT HAD BEGUN IN SPAIN IN MID-MAY, 2011.

THESE USED (+ ABUSED) ANARCHIST FORMS OF ORGANIZING. LIKE OCCUPY, THE 'SPANISH REVOLUTION WAS INSPIRED BY THE 'ARAB SPRING'.

UNLIKE THE 'ARAB SPRING,' OCCUPY IMPOSED PACIFISM + REFORMISM ON PARTICIPANTS AND ALSO LACKED GENUINE MASS MOBILIZATION.

MANY OF THE THOUSANDS THAT RALLIED OCT. 15 SOON LEFT AS OCCUPIERS BECAME BOGGED DOWN IN CREATING A NEW BUREAUCRACY.

IN N. AMERICA, THE MOST NOTABLE EXCEPTION TO THIS WAS OCCUPY OAKLAND, WHICH ALSO BECAME KNOWN AS THE OAKLAND COMMUNE.

IT STARTED ON OCT. 10 IN A PARK OUTSIDE OF OAKLAND CITY HALL DURING A NATIVE SOLIDARITY RALLY OF SEVERAL HUNDRED PEOPLE.

OAKLAND HAS A LONG HISTORY OF STRUGGLE (THE BLACK PANTHERS STARTED THERE) AND THE OCCUPY SITE HAD MORE RADICALS INVOLVED THAN IN MOST OTHER CITIES.

ON OCT. 25 AT 4:30AM HUNDREDS OF RIOT COPS MOVED IN TO EVICT THE COMMUNE, FIRING TEAR GAS + BATON ROUNDS. 79 PEOPLE WERE ARRESTED.

IN THE EVENING 1,500 PEOPLE RALLIED AGAINST THE POLICE VIOLENCE + THERE WERE MORE CLASHES.

AN IRAQ WAR VET- SCOTT OLSEN - WAS HIT WITH A POLICE PROJECTILE + SUFFERED A FRACTURED SKULL. HIS INJURY WOULD ANGER MANY...

THE NEXT DAY- OCT. 26- SOME 3000 RALLIED. THEY TORE DOWN FENCING COPS HAD ERECTED AROUND THE PARK + RE-OCCUPIED IT.

WHOSE PARK? OUR PARK!

THEY ALSO CALLED FOR A 1-DAY GENERAL STRIKE ON NOV. 2 IN RESPONSE TO THE REPRESSION.

ON NOV. 2, AS MANY AS 40,000 PEOPLE PARTICIPATED IN STRIKES + RALLIES IN OAKLAND.

SMASH!

AN ANTI-CAPITALIST MARCH OF 1,000 OR SO ATTACKED SEVERAL BANKS IN THE DOWNTOWN.

THE PORT OF OAKLAND, THE FIFTH BUSIEST IN ALL THE US, WAS BLOCKADED BY THOUSANDS AND COMPLETELY SHUT DOWN FOR THE DAY.

BLOCK CAPITALISM

KOJ OCCUPY

OCCUPY OAKLAND

THEN, ON NOV. 14, AS MANY AS 700-1,000 COPS MOVED IN AND AGAIN EVICTED THE COMMUNE.

DURING THIS TIME AS WELL, CIVIC OFFICIALS BEGAN EVICTING OCCUPY SITES ACROSS THE US + CANADA, INCL. OCCUPY WALL STREET.

HUNDREDS OF PEOPLE WERE ARRESTED AS COPS + CITY WORKERS TORE DOWN THE CAMPS.

SOME ATTEMPTED TO RE-OCCUPY CITY PARKS, BUT BY DECEMBER ALMOST ALL THE MAIN OCCUPY SITES WERE DISMANTLED.

DESPITE MOST PROTESTERS' PACIFIST METHODS THERE WAS WIDESPREAD POLICE VIOLENCE...

IN RESPONSE TO THE REPRESSION, OCCUPY OAKLAND CALLED FOR A SHUTDOWN OF ALL WEST COAST PORTS ON DEC. 12.

ON THAT DAY, BLOCKADES OCCURRED IN OAKLAND, PORTLAND, SEATTLE + VANCOUVER, COSTING INDUSTRY MILLIONS OF DOLLARS.

ALTHOUGH THE OCCUPY MOVEMENT WAS UNABLE TO SUSTAIN ITSELF OVER THE LONG TERM IT REVEALED A WIDESPREAD DESIRE FOR SOCIAL CHANGE + DISCONTENT WITH THE SYSTEM.

OPINION POLLS FROM NBC, CBS, + TIME SHOWED THAT AS MANY AS 54% OF US CITIZENS SUPPORTED THE VIEWS OF OCCUPY PROTESTERS.

WITH ECONOMIC CONDITIONS CONTINUING TO DECLINE... ...ANTI-CAPITALIST RESISTANCE CAN ONLY INCREASE.